TRUE CRIME: BRITISH KILLERS

A Prequel

JASON NEAL

Cover photos of:

Peter Bryan (top-left)

Levi Bellfield (top-right)

Steven Wright (bottom-left)

Tony Hardy (bottom-right)

Also by Jason Neal

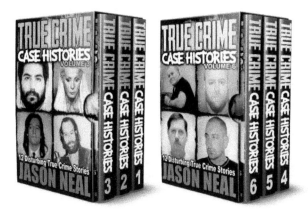

Looking for more true crime books?? I am constantly adding new volumes of True Crime Case Histories. All books are available in Kindle, paperback, hardcover, and audiobooks.

Check out the complete series on Amazon:

US: http://truecrime.page/amazonUS

UK: http://truecrime.page/amazonUK

Choose Your Free True Crime Audiobook

Add Audible Narration and Keep the Story Going!
Plus Get a FREE True Crime Audiobook!

Switch between listening to an audiobook and reading on your Kindle. **Plus choose your first audiobook for FREE!**

http://truecrime.page/AudibleUS

http://truecrime.page/AudibleUK

CONTENTS

NOTES FROM THE AUTHOR

Many of those who follow my work know that over the past years I have split my time between London and Arizona. Though we've loved living in the UK, this year my wife and I are leaving London and moving permanently to the US.

As these past few months have been my final months in London, I thought it would be fitting to write a book about some of the most notorious killers in UK history.

This book is not officially part of the True Crime Case Histories series, but it's written in a very similar style.

As with all of my previous books, I like to give the reader a quick word of warning. Most news articles and television true crime shows skim over the gruesome details in stories such as these. In these books I do extensive research and try not gloss over the facts. These books are not for the squeamish. My intention is to present the story as it was, regardless of how unsettling it may have been.

That being said, the research of these stories comes from many different sources which can be complex and varying.

Occasionally different sources may conflict with one another. I've done my best to analyze the sources and present them as a story that represents the truth as best I can.

I hope you enjoy reading this book as much as I've enjoyed researching and writing it.

- Jason

1

THE CAMDEN RIPPER

I n December 2002, fifty-one-year-old Tony Hardy's life had spiraled into an abyss of deviant sex, drugs, alcohol, and depression, but it hadn't always been that way.

Born in 1952, Tony was raised in a lower-middle-class family with his four siblings. His father had spent his life working in the gypsum mines of Staffordshire, England, and Tony was expected to do the same. At an early age Tony knew he was different. He knew he was destined for greatness and had a deep burning desire to make much more of himself than just a lowly laborer like his father.

Tony started off on the right foot. He knew that he would need to study hard if he wanted to make a better life for himself. He buried his nose in his books, excelled in school, and by his late teens was admitted to the Imperial College London. It was an elite school located just around the corner from Kensington Palace and Royal Albert Hall in the center of London, and is still considered one of the top universities in the world.

While attending college, Tony realized he was smarter than most of the other students: Much smarter. He believed that there were very few people that could match his intellect, and certainly not the police. However, he did meet a girl that he thought matched his intellect. Judith Dwight worked as a secretary at the school, and in 1972 they were married and immediately started a family, eventually having two girls and two boys.

While living in London, only a few miles from Whitechapel, Tony developed a fascination with the stories of Jack the Ripper, reading every book he could find about the notorious killer. Jack the Ripper was believed to be responsible for eleven heinous murders of prostitutes in the late 1800s in Whitechapel and was never caught. Hardy admired his ability to evade police and often thought Jack the Ripper must have been extremely intelligent as well.

His close friend Maureen Reeve later recounted his obsession with Jack the Ripper,

> "Anthony was obsessed with serial killers and we talked about them on several occasions. We had long discussions about Jack the Ripper, and Anthony thought he had a brilliant mind. He reckoned Jack the Ripper was a very clever bloke because he murdered all those prostitutes and never got caught. I never thought anything of it."

After graduation, Tony landed a high-paying job with British Sugar, one of the largest food manufacturers at the time, working as a mechanical engineer. He excelled at his work and quickly moved up the corporate ranks.

For a time, Tony and Judith had a normal happy marriage. They had their kids, but Tony needed more. He had an obsession with sadomasochistic and violent sex, and that was something that Judith couldn't provide for him. His extreme fetish led him to have affairs, but he eventually realized that it was much easier to just hire prostitutes.

In the mid-70s, the UK had a severe economic downturn and Tony lost his high-paying job. This was a severe blow to his already inflated ego. In his mind, someone of his superior intellect just didn't lose their job. This loss was hard on him and he fell into a deep depression suffering from severe mood swings and violent outbursts. Psychiatrists diagnosed him as bipolar and put him on medication, but his mental illness would dominate his life from that point forward.

By the late 70s Hardy got a new high-paying engineering job in Tasmania, Australia. This was exciting for him and his family, but it didn't solve any of their problems. Now in his late twenties, he was still suffering with his disorder as well as his desire for more and more violent sex.

In 1982 the economy was in a recession and Hardy was let go from his job once again due to job cuts. This news ignited his anger, and he began to unleash his violent behavior on his wife and kids.

At the height of his depression, but still knowing he was much more intelligent than law enforcement, Hardy believed he could commit the perfect crime. He wanted to get rid of his wife, but didn't want to go through the hassle of a divorce. He filled a two-liter plastic bottle with water, put it in the freezer and let it turn into a solid block of ice. He then took the rock-hard piece of ice and beat his wife over the head with it while she slept. Hardy believed it would be the perfect weapon. Once thawed, the murder weapon would completely disappear.

But murder was a lot more difficult than he expected. He planned on beating her unconscious and drowning her in the tub to make it look like she slipped in the tub, hit her head, and drowned. But he didn't count on her staying conscious. Not only did she stay conscious, she fought back. Hardy only stopped when one of his children came into the room and started screaming.

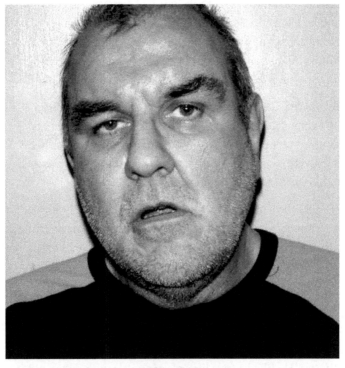

Anthony Hardy

Police arrested Hardy, but domestic violence was looked upon differently in the eighties. Despite openly admitting that he was trying to kill his wife, in Tasmania the offense was not considered attempted murder, but only a domestic abuse issue. Regardless, the offense still required a jail sentence.

Hardy convinced authorities that, because of his mental illness, he should be locked up in a mental hospital rather than a jail. He later told friends that it was all an act to avoid a jail term. While in the psych unit in Queensland, Hardy played the game and cooperated with hospital authorities and was eventually released.

When Hardy was released from the psychiatric hospital, he was deported back to the United Kingdom. He had attempted to kill his wife, but was now still a free man, which reinforced his belief that he could outwit anyone. Just like Jack the Ripper.

His wife and kids had already moved back to the United Kingdom, and Judith had filed for divorce. This infuriated him.

Hardy had gone from a well-paid executive to a homeless alcoholic sleeping in various hostels throughout the London area. He was obsessed with his now ex-wife and stalked her, even planting microphones in her home so he could listen to her conversations.

Judith pleaded with police that her ex-husband was endangering the lives of herself and her children, and she was granted a restraining order. But a piece of paper didn't stop Hardy. He quickly broke the restraining order, which landed him with a short prison sentence.

After Hardy was released from prison, he moved to the Camden area of London so he could be near King's Cross Station. The King's Cross area was known throughout the nineties as a red-light district of London with plenty of pimps, pushers and prostitutes.

Hardy frequently hired prostitutes from the streets of King's Cross, looking for vulnerable women to satisfy his deviant sexual needs. He was known among the regular girls in the area for his need of violent sex as well as his stench. Hardy rarely bathed or changed his clothes.

In 1998, a sex worker accused him of rape, claiming he was trying to kill her. Unfortunately for the girl, rape is hard to prove when the claim comes from a prostitute that's being paid for sex. Her claims were ignored by police, and Hardy had once again evaded arrest. Though his life had been in a constant downward spiral, he still believed himself to be invincible.

Hardy was known by his neighbors as the local nut case. His neighbors knew he would often bring prostitutes to his home, and they were aware of his addictions and mental issues. They were also aware of his obsession with Jack the Ripper—Hardy would constantly talk about him. But for the most part his neighbors thought he was just annoying, strange, and a bit mentally ill, but overall harmless. None of them imagined he would be capable of murder.

In January 2002 Hardy had a dispute with his upstairs neighbor. He claimed that her shower was leaking water into his flat, but she refused to do anything about it, Hardy took matters into his own hands. While the woman was away from her home, he painted "Fuck you Slut" on her front door. At the bottom he signed it with the letter "T." He then poured battery acid through the mail slot in the door, spilling it all over the door and the ground outside.

As he left the scene, Hardy stepped in the spilled battery acid. It didn't take much for police to find him. They simply followed the footprints straight to Hardy's door.

When police confronted him, Hardy invited them into his home; he was nonchalant and unapologetic. He freely admitted that he had graffitied her door and poured the battery acid so police arrested him for the vandalism. As the officers looked around his cluttered, unkempt apartment, they noticed a locked bedroom door and asked him to open it. Hardy claimed he couldn't, that it was the door to his roommate's bedroom, and he didn't have the key.

His roommate, thirty-one-year-old Sally Rose White, was a developmentally challenged young woman with a history of running away from home. She was working as a prostitute in the King's Cross area to pay for her crack cocaine addiction.

As police were taking Hardy into custody, they told him to grab his coat. Before allowing him to put on the coat, police searched the pockets and realized Hardy had lied to them. Inside his coat pocket, they found the key to the locked room.

When police opened the bedroom door, they were shocked to find the naked body of a deceased woman lying on the bed —it was his roommate, Sally Rose White. There was damage to the top of her head, blood on the sheets, and on the floor was a hoodie with a large blood stain inside the hood. A trail of blood was on the wall at the head of the bed, as if her head had slid down the wall. Her face was covered with a cloth, and there was a bite mark on her right thigh.

Sally's body had been posed near a rubber Satan mask, several crucifixes, and a single black high-heeled shoe; a dildo was protruding from her vagina. Photo equipment was set up around the bed as if in preparation for a photoshoot. Near the door was a bucket of soapy water with a sponge. The water in the bucket was still warm.

In Hardy's living room, police found three televisions and several stacks of VHS porn tapes totaling over seventy, mostly of sadistic porn that depicted simulated rape.

Hardy denied knowing anything about Sally's body and why it was there, but it was clear to the police what had happened and they arrested Hardy on suspicion of murder.

After his arrest, Freddy Patel, an experienced pathologist, performed the postmortem examination. To the frustration of police, Patel found that Sally Rose White had died of congenital heart failure, not from the wound on the top of her head.

Despite the wound on her head, the blood trail down the wall, the blood-soaked hoodie that had been removed after death, the positioning of the body with a satanic mask, the insertion of a dildo into her vagina, the photographic equipment, her head being covered, and the bucket of warm soapy water, the pathologist still insisted that no crime had been committed. Investigators demanded that Patel re-examine her, but even after he had performed a second postmortem examination, Patel insisted she had died of natural causes.

This infuriated investigators, but they had no choice. If the pathologist said there was no murder, there was nothing to investigate. They had to drop the charges. They charged Hardy for the vandalism, but again he convinced authorities that his mental illness was to blame and he spent time in a hospital rather than jail.

Hardy was sectioned under the Mental Health Act to St. Luke's Hospital near Camden. Again, he cooperated with doctors and psychiatrists, but didn't let them know of his true sick desires.

During his stay in the mental hospital Hardy's psychiatrists wrote six warnings that he was vulnerable to relapse, posed a high risk of violence, and that women and prostitutes were at a particular risk. The doctors wrote that Hardy had a personality disorder that had not been treated, claiming,

> "There is strong evidence of risk of re-offending and he is likely to cause others serious physical or psychological harm."

Despite all the warnings, in November 2002, after only eleven months in the hospital, a panel of three released him. The panel argued that Hardy was "mentally ill", but had a "natural human right to be treated in the surroundings which will encourage and support his own efforts." Additionally, the Mental Health Trust didn't alert the police or his neighbors of his release. He was once again a free man, reinforcing his belief that he was invincible.

During his stay in the mental hospital Hardy had become even more obsessed with drugs, alcohol, porn, and prostitutes. His behavior after his release became increasingly strange. He began writing letters to prostitutes asking for dominant sex, claiming he was independently wealthy and looking for a "special relationship."

He was also known to take photos of women in Camden bars and would lick the leather of sofas and chairs where the women had been sitting. In late December he walked into a church and asked members to pray for his immortal soul. But most disturbing of all, he had an overwhelming need to emulate his hero, Jack the Ripper.

Elizabeth Valad was a stunning brunette with a half-Iranian background. While in her early teens, Elizabeth started hanging around the wrong crowd and by the time she was sixteen she had dropped out of school and moved to London. She often told her mother she was working as a secretary, but in today's terms she would be known as a "sugar baby."

Elizabeth met a multi-millionaire in his seventies who kept an upscale flat for her in Chelsea, one of the most expensive areas of London. For ten years she lived off of the generosity of her benefactor, often referring to him as her "meal ticket." He supplied her with designer clothes, a new Mercedes, and they often dined together at the Ritz Carlton.

By 2001, however, Elizabeth was twenty-nine years old and her meal ticket had run out. She was on her own, and it wasn't long before she became addicted to drugs and resorted to street prostitution in the King's Cross area.

Just before Christmas 2002, Elizabeth Valad took to the streets of London and was never seen alive again.

On December 30, 2002, at about 3:00 a.m. a homeless man was rummaging through a dumpster behind a pub in Camden when he felt something cold and slimy inside a plastic garbage bag. He described it as feeling like two filets of salmon. When he opened the bag, it took him a minute to realize what he was looking at. What he had felt were the calf muscles from two female lower legs. Someone had sawed the legs off at the knees. When police arrived, they found a second garbage bag in the same dumpster containing a partial female torso.

Investigators taped off the area behind the pub and began searching the rest of the dumpsters in the immediate area, but found no more body parts. At dawn they began searching the dumpsters and drains of the entire surrounding area.

After searching for almost three days, in another dumpster less than 100 yards away they found more green garbage bags with female body parts, plus another partial torso, a right arm, a left arm, a foot, and a bloodstained bra. This second location served as the dumpster of the building where Anthony Hardy lived.

Bag filled with body parts

As the days went by, police widened their search around Camden and continued to find more garbage bags with more body parts. The Regent's Canal was also nearby. That was where the body of Paula Fields had been found the prior year. (See "The Canal Killer" in True Crime Case Histories Volume 3)

From the parts they had found, they knew there were two female victims, but the heads and hands of both were still missing. Police arranged scuba teams to dredge the canals looking for more parts, but found nothing.

There was also the possibility that trash collectors may have already picked up some parts from dumpsters and taken them to the landfill. A team of eighty officers would spend the next three weeks searching through endless tons of rubbish at the landfill, but again found nothing.

It was only a matter of time before police realized that some of the body parts were found at the same building that they found a dead body less than a year prior. Tony Hardy immediately became suspect number one. It had only been seven weeks since they had released Hardy from the mental hospital.

Police brought a large team of officers to Hardy's flat intending to break the door down, but there was no need. The door was slightly open, and they simply walked in, but there was no sign of Tony Hardy.

Inside Hardy's flat, the cement floors, walls, and doors were painted with nonsensical graffiti. The second bedroom where the body had been found before was again closed and locked. Hardy had wedged a gray set of tracksuit bottoms into the gap underneath the door. Investigators soon realized that the tracksuit was there to keep the smell of decomposition from escaping.

On the floor of the bedroom, investigators found a large black plastic garbage bag wrapped in twine. Inside the bag was a dismembered female torso. A hacksaw and three knives had been arranged neatly on the top of the bag. Small bits of flesh still hung from the teeth of the hacksaw blade. Police also found rubber gloves and an electric saw. There was also evidence that someone had taken photos at the scene.

Though it was obvious that he had dismembered the bodies there, police still used Luminol to document the presence of human blood. Luminol is a chemical that when sprayed upon a surface will react with the hemoglobin in traces of blood causing it to glow, even after attempts to clean the blood. When police sprayed the Luminol, Hardy's entire apartment lit up like a Christmas tree, particularly around the bathtub.

Fifty-one-year-old Tony Hardy always said he would be famous, and now he was. Police alerted the media that they were looking for him; they distributed photos and a description. The media dubbed Hardy the Camden Ripper.

When questioning neighbors, many recalled hearing sounds of an electric saw and the smell of incense coming from Hardy's apartment, but at the time they dismissed it, thinking their crazy neighbor was doing construction work in the middle of the night.

Hardy was on the run, but he didn't venture very far. Police received several reports that people had seen him around the Camden area, doing very little to disguise his appearance. Inside his flat they found his diabetes, bipolar, and manic depression medications. Hardy needed seven different kinds of medication and they knew he couldn't survive for long without it, so they alerted the nearby hospitals to be on the lookout for him.

Detectives then sifted through hours of security camera footage from the Camden area. On several cameras throughout the city, they could see Hardy opening dumpsters and casually throwing bags in. In some videos Hardy would look directly into the camera, as if he believed it was impossible for him to get caught.

Anthony Hardy w/photo equipment and NY Yankees hat

Investigators also found that Hardy regularly used a loyalty card at the local Sainsbury grocery store. The security cameras from his local store showed him using his loyalty card when buying the garbage bags that were used to deposit the body parts.

On January 2, 2003, an off-duty police officer spotted Anthony Hardy at the Great Ormond Street Hospital. When Hardy realized someone had spotted him, he ran. Two police officers gave chase and caught up with him, but Hardy was a very large man and fought back. He stabbed one officer in the hand and punched him, dislodging an eye from its socket. He punched the second officer and knocked him out completely. They called more police in to help, who pinned him down and apprehended him.

During the analysis of the female torso that had been found on the floor of the bedroom, they found that the victim had both breast and butt implants. Using the serial number on the butt implant, investigators identified her. It was twenty-nine-year-old Elizabeth Valad.

Elizabeth Valad

On January 3, using DNA, police were able to identify the second victim as Brigette MacClennan. Bridgette was a thirty-four-year-old mother of two, who was also a habitual drug user and a prostitute who worked the streets near King's Cross station.

Brigette MacClennan

Detectives interrogated Hardy for seventy-two hours, but he was defiant and said nothing other than "No comment."

It was clear from items in the bedroom that Hardy had taken photos of the killings, but they had no idea where the photos were and Hardy wasn't about to tell them. A few weeks after his arrest, a nearby photo processing center alerted police that they had two rolls of film that Hardy had dropped off for processing. Hardy had told the processing center that it was pornographic with consenting adults, but the photos clearly were more than that. Pathologists confirmed that the victims in the photos were dead when the photos were taken.

In over forty photos Hardy had covered the victims face with the red devil mask and his New York Yankees baseball hat—

the same hat he had been seen wearing in several of the security camera videos and on the day he was arrested. He had posed the bodies in pornographic poses with crucifixes and a dildo in their vaginas.

Before the trial Hardy refused to answer any questions at all. The only question he answered was where he had put the heads and hands of the girls. His reply was that he was too drunk and couldn't remember where he dumped them.

Hardy pleaded not guilty and was due to stand trial in November 2003 at the Old Bailey Central Criminal Court in London. The witnesses were prepped, and evidence was ready to present to the court. Then, on the first day of trial, Hardy suddenly changed his plea to guilty to all three counts of murder.

Anthony Hardy was given three life sentences. One for each life he took, although it's speculated that he may have killed more. The hands and heads of Elizabeth Valad and Brigette MacClennan were never found. At his sentencing the judge told Hardy,

"Only you know for sure how your victims met their deaths but the unspeakable indignities to which you subjected the bodies of your last two victims in order to satisfy your depraved and perverted needs are in no doubt."

Pathologist Freddy Patel, who twice determined Sally Rose White's death was due to natural causes, was in the news again in 2009.

During the G20 summit in London, thousands of protesters gathered in the city center while police set up roadblocks to control the crowds. An innocent newspaper vendor and father of nine, Ian Tomlinson, was not a protestor, but only trying to make his way home that evening and police mistook him for a protestor. He was bitten on the leg by a police dog, hit on the back of the legs with a baton and shoved to the ground by a police officer. He later died from an injury he sustained during the fall.

Freddy Patel was the first to examine the body of Ian Tomlinson. Patel's findings from that examination mistakenly determined that Tomlinson died of a heart attack. Subsequent examinations determined that Tomlinson died from internal bleeding from the injuries inflicted by police. An inquest jury found that Tomlinson had been unlawfully killed.

Patel was charged with sixty-eight failings of the examination. Among those was the fact that he had failed to include information about the internal bleeding. Patel was found to be "misleading, dishonest and liable to bring his profession into disrepute." He was also found to be "irresponsible" with the postmortem examination of Sally Rose White. In 2012 Freddy Patel was taken off the medical registry for these failures and failures found on three additional postmortem examinations.

―――

In 2005 through letters written to his friends from his cell at Wakefield Prison in Yorkshire, Anthony Hardy professed that he prays for his own forgiveness and was "finding God" and had "rediscovered Catholicism."

> "I have prayed for forgiveness virtually every day for the past
> year since my brother died in a car accident in Australia aged

60 on January 20, 2003. God has taken him to be with other members of my family. The chaplain of the prison gave me the news, and we prayed together about Terry (his brother) and myself."

In another letter Hardy wrote,

"Elaine (his lawyer) brought me the news that Harold Shipman had hanged himself on Monday night. I wonder if he redeemed himself before he died (repented?). 'I am the resurrection and the life for whosoever believes me shall live, even though he dies' said the Lord! John 11.25. Shipman didn't adhere to his hippocratic oath, so I leave his fate to the almighty. Amen."

He continued,

"I went to Rampton Hospital between April and July 2003 for assessment and met another wonderful chaplain and went to services when staff allowed me. I wanted to join the choir, but circumstances and my return have prevented it."

Despite his newfound religion, prison authorities reprimanded Hardy for trying to write the number "666" into his date of birth.

"The 'authorities' think I'm behaving badly rather than being ill. I've lost all my correspondence due to a flood of biblical proportions which I caused in my cell. There's a verse in the Bible which says 'and wash away all your iniquities' and that's what I did in the flood! The staff were not so forgiving! I've become a Catholic since moving to Wakefield but they have no catholic priest to hear my confession, instruct me in the catechism, or help me atone for my sins, so I'm in limbo until September when a priest will be appointed."

"I'm going to ask Elaine to write to my ex-wife and tell her about my rediscovered faith and assure her that she is safe now. I don't expect I will ever be released from prison. I'd like to know how many grandchildren I have. I expect there are several."

"It's lovely to have someone to write to who is my intellectual equal. There are many asylum seekers in Belmarsh and people who have been persecuted for their beliefs. Several are friends of mine and, of course, I have Christian friends from all parts of the world. Very few have had the benefit of an excellent education though."

"I do art here which I find very satisfying. I'm in my Anthony van Dyck phase now. I have his type of beard, but my favourite artist is Salvador Dali. I've become a vegan. Can you put me in touch with the Vegan Society? The prison can't, even though they provide a vegan diet. I'm trying to lose weight by not eating fat in meat and dairy products."

"I can't get to education either (High Security Category!) so I write short stories for my own amusement and read psychology, science, and literature when I can. I have been to the gym here and in Rampton, where I played volleyball quite successfully. Rampton had a pool, so when I dived in the water dived out!! Seriously they had a good music system at the pool so I had a good one-hour session once a week."

"I'm waiting to be given a tariff by the judge which could take months. There are 700 lifer cases waiting to be dealt with."

In 2012 Anthony Hardy's sentence was given a whole life tariff, meaning he will never be released from prison, a rare sentence in the United Kingdom.

2

THE LONDON CANNIBAL

In the United States, a life sentence generally means that the offender will spend the rest of their life in prison with no hope of parole. The sentence has a very different meaning in the United Kingdom. A killer can be convicted of a heinous murder and still be released in as little as eight to ten years as I've highlighted in other UK crime stories. The decision of parole is usually up to the judge presiding over the case. The story of Peter Bryan highlights the tragic failures of Britain's healthcare and justice systems.

Peter Bryan was born in London on October 4, 1969, to immigrant parents from Barbados. Bryan grew up in East London and dropped out of school at the age of fourteen. He began working in a street stall where he sold clothes and later taught cooking lessons at a London homeless shelter.

When he was eighteen, Bryan was arguing with another resident of his apartment building one evening when the two started fighting. Bryan tried to throw the man through a sixth-floor window of the building, but was unsuccessful. The police were called to break up the fight, and Bryan was left with a huge gash on his face that left him permanently scarred. The man told the police that the attack was completely unprovoked, but no charges were filed and the police took no action against either party.

By the time he was twenty-three, Bryan was working as a shop assistant at an upscale clothing boutique in the fashionable Chelsea borough of London. While working there Bryan developed a crush on the owner's twenty-year-old daughter, Nisha Sheth, but Nisha had no interest in Bryan and continually turned down his advances.

In early March 1993 Bryan was caught stealing clothes from the shop and was promptly fired by Nisha's father. The combined anger of Nisha's rejection and being caught stealing enraged him and a week later on March 18, 1993 he came back to the shop to get revenge.

Bryan burst into the shop brandishing a claw hammer and screaming at Nisha. Nisha's twelve-year-old brother Bobby gallantly tried to protect his big sister, but Bryan easily knocked the boy to the floor. Bryan then set his sights on Nisha. As she grabbed the phone to try to call for help, Bryan pounded her repeatedly over the head with the claw hammer while her little brother watched in horror. Nisha didn't stand a chance; she died from her head wounds before the ambulance arrived.

Bryan fled the scene and ran across the River Thames to the nearby Battersea neighborhood. He smoked a joint to try to calm his nerves, entered a building and jumped from the third floor. Bryan survived his suicide attempt and was arrested for the murder of Nisha Sheth.

Ultimately Bryan pleaded guilty to the charge of manslaughter on the grounds of diminished responsibility. In 1994 he was sentenced to the Rampton maximum security psychiatric unit in northern England. Officially the term of his sentence was "without limit of time." The judge left the length of the sentence to be decided upon by the psychiatrists treating him.

Peter Bryan

During the early years of his stay in the psychiatric ward his doctors described him as "unpredictable," "extremely dangerous," and "a grave risk to others." Over time, however, their opinion of Bryan's demeanor changed. By February 2001, after being in maximum security for almost eight years, mental health experts believed he could interact with the public again. The staff believed he had made considerable progress in "behavior, attitude, maturity, relationship, anger, and insight." They believed he could live within the community, but he would still need supervision.

Bryan was transferred to the Johnson Howard Centre in Hackney, East London. Normally a mental patient would have been required to stay two full years in transition, but doctors believed so adamantly in Bryan's progress that he was only required to stay for a six month trial period.

Just nine years after he brazenly hammered a girl to death, a mental health review tribunal approved Bryan for a move to Riverside Hostel, a low-security facility in North London. He was given a key to the building and was allowed to come and go as he pleased.

During his brief stay at Riverside Hostel, staff caught Bryan blowing raspberries on a sixteen-year-old girl's stomach. The girl's infuriated parents threatened him and considered the act to be sexual harassment. Bryan's doctors, worried for his safety, requested yet another transfer.

By late 2003 psychiatrists stated that Bryan had shown "a continued improvement in his mental state" and that he "did not present any major risks." He was approved for a transfer to the Newham General Hospital under the supervision of a psychiatrist who had no experience working with a killer, and he was assigned a social worker who had been working only five months and had no experience of mental health patients at all. Again, Bryan was allowed to come and go as he pleased.

In January 2004 the inexperienced social worker wrote a letter to the Home Office stating that he had no further concerns about Peter Bryan and suggested that he be moved to a "low support accommodation."

The day before his transfer Bryan wrote a letter to a friend saying,

"I still have an ACE card to play. I can still play my best card of all."

On February 17, 2004 Bryan was moved to the Topaz Ward of Newham General Hospital, a ward with almost no supervision at all, allowing him complete freedom to leave the facility. Bryan was now officially considered a "voluntary patient."

Within three hours of his transfer, Peter Bryan left the building and went to the nearest hardware store. There he purchased a claw hammer, a box cutter, and a screwdriver. He then entered the ground-floor flat of his friend Brian Cherry in nearby Walthamstow.

After complaints of screams coming from Cherry's flat, his neighbor Nicola Newman let herself in. She was immediately hit with the smell of disinfectant. Peter Bryan walked into the hallway to greet her, shirtless and holding a kitchen knife. Bryan said, "Brian is dead."

Nicola didn't believe him and walked into the living room. There she saw Brian Cherry's naked body on the floor with one of his arms detached from his body. She immediately ran home to call the police.

When police arrived, they found the dismembered body of forty-three-year-old Brian Cherry lying on the living room floor in a pool of blood. Both of Cherry's arms and one leg were lying nearby, detached from his body. A claw hammer, box cutter, and a kitchen knife were lying on the floor near the body. In the kitchen, Peter Bryan was covered in dried blood and had a kitchen knife in his hand. On the stove was a hot frying pan with meat in it and a tub of butter on the counter. A cutting board with clumps of meat, blood, and hair lay next to the sink.

"I ate his brain with butter. It was really nice," Bryan told police.

Brian Cherry's head had been crushed by the claw hammer with at least twenty-four blows, and his head had been partially cut off. Police had interrupted Bryan before he had a chance to complete the amputation of the second leg and the head.

When arrested Bryan claimed he was, "comforted by the smell of blood."

"I used the Stanley knife to cut them off and some other kitchen knives but I had to stamp on them to break the bone."

Brian Cherry's twenty-year-old niece said,

"It's like something out of a horror film. My uncle was a totally kind and gentle man. Both his hands were broken when he tried to defend himself. Parts of his body were not even identifiable. He obviously didn't stand a chance."

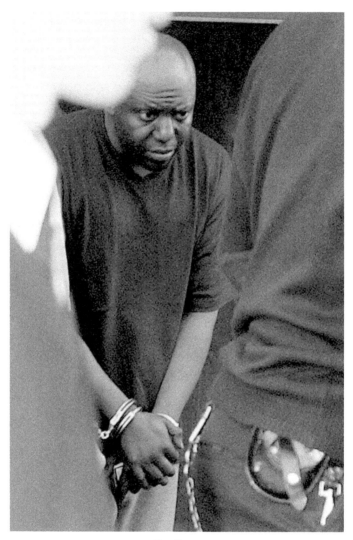

Peter Bryan

Two months later, on April 15, 2004, Bryan was admitted to the Broadmoor maximum security hospital, a notorious prison for the criminally insane. In another massive failure of the health system, within days of his arrival doctors believed Bryan had "settled" and he was transferred to a medium-risk ward within the prison.

Richard Loudwell was another inmate in the medium-risk ward of the prison. The sixty-year-old was admitted to Broadmoor that January and was awaiting trial for the murder of an eighty-two-year-old woman. Loudwell had complained to prison staff that he was being bullied by other inmates. His family had tried to help him and complained to the prison staff that they were worried for his safety, but the complaints were ignored.

A senior nurse at Broadmoor commented that Loudwell was one of the

> "…most unpopular patients I have ever met. It was inevitable that sooner or later he would be assaulted."

Just ten days after Peter Bryan had been admitted to Broadmoor, he saw Richard Loudwell in the dining room of the ward, removed the cord from his own trousers and used it to strangle Loudwell. He wrapped the cord around his neck and violently beat his head against the floor. Loudwell was rushed to hospital but died from his injuries a month later.

During interviews with his psychiatrists, Bryan said,

> "I've had these urges towards him for a long time. I was just waiting for my chance to get at him. He's the bottom of the food chain, old, haggard… he looked like he's had his innings."

> "I intended to kill him as quickly as possible, but gave up because I became tired."

"I would have done someone else if you hadn't come along. I wanted their souls. I didn't have much time. If I did, I'd have tried to cook him and eat him."

On March 15, 2005, Peter Bryan pleaded guilty at Old Bailey Central Criminal Court to two additional counts of manslaughter on the grounds of diminished responsibility.

During the trial Judge Giles Forrester stated:

"You killed on these last two occasions because it gave you a thrill and a feeling of power when you ate flesh. Although substantially impaired, you do of course bear criminal responsibility. The violence on each occasion was extreme and unpredictable, accompanied by bizarre and sexual overtones."

Bryan was sentenced to two life terms and is unlikely to ever be released.

In 2009, the National Health System published two lengthy reports of the extreme failures of the health system. The first report dealt with the death of Brian Cherry,

"There was no particular failure by any individual professional."

"He did not display the expected signs of schizophrenia and appeared to behave normally even when seriously mentally unwell."

"Other than a couple of minor incidents during his early years at Rampton, Peter Bryan had not displayed any signs of aggressive behaviour since he killed Nisha Sheth. Bryan was able to manipulate his care regime."

The second report covered the killing of Richard Loudwell. In this report, the National Health Service was much more critical of the Broadmoor facility. Bryan had only been there for ten days and was allowed unsupervised access despite nine employees being on duty at the time.

> "No single individual, whether patient or member of staff, was responsible for the death of Richard Loudwell. There were in our view deficiencies in many aspects of the care provided to both Richard Loudwell and Peter Bryan and shortcomings at every level within the Trust. It was the combination of these shortcomings that led to Richard Loudwell"s death."

Ultimately, no action was taken against any hospital staff. Peter Bryan still resides at the Broadmoor facility and will stay there for the rest of his days.

3

THE ACID BATH KILLER

The story of John George Haigh is notoriously known as one of the most gruesome stories in British history. His killings were driven strictly by his own greed.

John Haigh was born in 1909 in Stamford, Lincolnshire in central England. He had a particularly strange childhood, raised by ultra-conservative parents that belonged to the Plymouth Brethren church. The Plymouth Brethren believe that the Bible represents the supreme authority of all things. Their strict religion deprived John of things that other kids enjoyed, like sports, Christmas and entertainment of all kinds. Any variance from the doctrine came with the fierce threat of eternal damnation.

John was a bright young child and at the age of ten he received a scholarship to a private catholic school in Wakefield for his music abilities. Though he excelled academically, he was a mischievous boy and loved to play tricks on friends and teachers. His school years were plagued with petty crimes, and on several occasions he was caught forging his teachers' signatures on school documents.

Haigh, an only child, had no interest in his parents' religion, and wanted a life outside of the small coal-mining village where he was raised. At seventeen, an ambitious Haigh left home to work as a motor engineer. He believed himself to be the entrepreneurial type, but had no intention of going about things in a conventional manner. His first business venture was selling cars that didn't belong to him by forging vehicle documents.

Haigh was well-dressed, well-mannered, cheerful and charming. His persona was a perfect match for his fraudulent scams.

At twenty-five Haigh got married, but the marriage only lasted a few months when his wife found out that his business ventures were a sham. It wasn't long before he was arrested and sentenced to fifteen months in prison for fraud and forgery.

John Haigh

By 1936 Haigh had moved to London and got a job with a wealthy man named William McSwan, who owned a chain of amusement arcades and many properties throughout London. Haigh worked as the family's personal chauffeur and maintained the pinball machines in their arcades. Haigh admired McSwan's wealthy lifestyle, and the two became very good friends, but they lost touch when Haigh was hauled away to prison again.

When released from prison, Haigh was still determined to make his fortune on his own. He posed as a lawyer and created a fictitious pseudonym calling himself William Cato Adamson. He made a nice living selling fraudulent shares of the estates of recently deceased people, but was caught when he misspelled the city of Guildford as "Guilford" in one of his advertisements. Someone suspected that a real, educated lawyer wouldn't make such a simple misspelling. This mistake landed him in jail yet again. Between 1934 and 1943,

Haigh went to prison three times for various fraud and theft crimes.

During his time in prison, Haigh spent much of his time reading books. He wanted to learn the British legal system and was in search of the perfect crime. One particular crime that intrigued him was a murder from 1925 in France. Georges-Alexandre Sarret had killed two people and used sulfuric acid to dissolve the bodies. Sarret was eventually caught and sent to the guillotine, but Haigh believed he could do it much better and not get caught. He mistakenly believed that in Britain, if there's no body, then they can't prosecute a person for murder.

While in Lincoln prison, Haigh worked in the tinsmith factory and gained access to sulfuric acid. He bribed his fellow inmates with cigarettes to bring him mice that he could experiment with. He would drop the mice into jars of sulfuric acid to determine the exact quantity and time needed to make a human body completely disappear.

In 1943, Haigh was released from prison a third time and worked in the Kensington neighborhood of London as an accountant at an engineering firm. One evening after work Haigh was at the Goat Pub on Kensington High Street when he ran into his old friend William McSwan. Haigh was introduced to McSwan's parents, who also owned several properties throughout London and lived off of the rents they produced. Over drinks they discussed the prospect of Haigh working for the family collecting the rents from their properties. They also discussed the war that was currently raging throughout Europe. Conscription (known as "the draft" in the US) was happening in the United Kingdom and McSwan was of an age to be drafted for the war. The McSwans were desperately looking for a way for their son to avoid going to war.

On September 6, 1944, McSwan told Haigh that some of his pinball machines needed some work and Haigh invited him to his basement workshop at 79 Gloucester Road just opposite the Gloucester tube station. Haigh was excited to test his acid experiment on an actual human.

Once Haigh had lured his friend to his basement workshop, he struck McSwan over the head with a heavy metal pipe. Haigh had already prepared for the event and had purchased carboys full of sulfuric acid and a metal oil drum.

He put on his protective equipment, which consisted of a rubber raincoat, thick rubber gloves, thigh-high rubber boots and a wartime gas mask to protect himself from the toxic acid fumes.

Once McSwan was dead, Haigh tipped the barrel on its side and folded up his body into it. He raised the barrel upright again and began pouring the acid into the barrel over McSwan's body. Haigh needed the body to completely disappear.

As the body was dissolving in the acid, Haigh contacted McSwan's parents, Amy and Donald McSwan. He explained that he had found a way for William to avoid being sent to war and had sent him to Scotland to stay in hiding. The McSwans were upset that they didn't get to say goodbye to their son, but ultimately they were happy that he had avoided going to war and would contact him when it was over.

Two days later when William's body was completely dissolved by the acid, Haigh poured the gooey sludge down the floor drain of his Gloucester Road basement workshop and the remains flowed through the sewers of London into the River Thames.

With William out of the way, Haigh became close friends with Amy and Donald McSwan. He took over William's duties of collecting the rents from their properties and helped them run all of their business dealings.

Haigh became an integral part of their business for the next ten months until he gave them some good news. The war was ending and William would be coming home for a surprise visit. On July 2, 1945, Haigh informed Amy and Donald that William was back in London and waiting for them at his Gloucester Road workshop.

As he did with William, once they were in his basement, Haigh clubbed both of them over the head with an iron bar and prepared their acid baths. Again, the acid sludge of the two bodies went down the basement drain into the Thames.

Once the entire McSwan family had been eliminated, Haigh took over the entire family business. Using his forgery skills, Haigh faked documents to show that the McSwans had immigrated to the United States. He sold their properties as his own and pocketed the money. Haigh was now a wealthy man, but he didn't know how to handle the money. He lived in expensive hotels, bought luxury cars and spent unwisely. The wealth that the McSwans had taken a lifetime building was spent by Haigh in only three short years.

By 1947 Haigh was broke again and needed new victims, when he met Archibald and Rose Henderson. The Hendersons were a wealthy couple who owned several flats and a shop in London. Haigh answered an ad they had placed to sell a London house and when Mrs. Henderson learned that

Haigh played piano she invited him to play for them at their housewarming party.

By that time Haigh no longer had the basement workshop on Gloucester Road. He had a tiny, one-room workshop on Leopold Road in Crawley, forty miles south of London.

Haigh had led the Hendersons to believe that he ran a successful engineering factory in Crawley and proposed a joint venture with the couple. On February 12, 1948, he invited Archibald to his small workshop.

Once inside the workshop, Haigh shot Archibald in the head with a revolver that he had stolen from their own home. Before he prepared the acid bath, he needed to take care of Rose as well. Haigh traveled back to London to tell her that her husband had taken ill in Crawley and she needed to come to him immediately. Once inside his workshop, he shot Rose and prepared the oil drums.

The major difference between the Gloucester Road basement and the new workshop on Leopold Road was that the Crawley location didn't have a floor drain. Haigh's only option to dispose of the acid was to wheel the drums into the yard that surrounded the workshop and pour the sludge into a corner of the yard. In the basement, all remains disappeared forever, but in the yard, there was a small amount of sludge residue. But Haigh felt confident that he would never get caught, as long as there was no body to prove that a murder had taken place.

Haigh used his forgery skills once again to make it seem as if the Hendersons had moved to South Africa. He then sold their properties, but the money he made only lasted him another year before he was broke once again.

Haigh had been living in South Kensington at the Onslow Court Hotel for the past four years. The hotel was known as a home for a much older clientele, but that's exactly what Haigh wanted. He needed a new victim—preferably a rich, older woman.

Mrs. Olivia Durand-Deacon was a sixty-nine-year-old widow who had been living in the hotel for the past six years. Despite her age, Mrs. Durand-Deacon still had an entrepreneurial spirit and let Haigh know of her idea to make artificial fingernails out of plastic. She told him that she had £36,000 in stocks that her late husband had left her to invest in her new venture. When Haigh heard her idea and the amount of money she was sitting on, he knew he had the perfect victim.

He explained to her that he had an engineering workshop in Crawley that could produce the artificial nails for her, and he would love to show it to her. He offered to drive her down to Crawley in his fancy Alvis sports car.

Mrs. Durand-Deacon fell for his convincing charm, dressed up in her finest jewelry and furs, and on February 18, 1949, she made the drive down to Crawley with Haigh.

Mrs. Durand-Deacon must have been shocked to learn that she was wearing her finest furs to visit such a grimy little workshop, but she would have been even more shocked when she realized Haigh's only intention was to kill her. Once inside the workshop he shot her in the back of the head with the same .38 caliber handgun that he had stolen from the Archibalds.

He then took the fur and jewelry off of her body, crumpled her body into a barrel, and poured the acid over her. Haigh calmly walked around the corner to a 14th century medieval restaurant called The Ancient Priors, where he calmly ordered an egg on toast with tea and had a chat with the owner while the body dissolved.

After his lunch, Haigh returned to the workshop and poured the remains of Mrs. Durand-Deacon into the yard. That evening he drove back to London to the Onslow Court Hotel. What Haigh hadn't accounted for was her close friend Mrs. Constance Lane, who had known about her friends' trip to Crawley with Haigh and was anxiously awaiting her return.

Mrs. Lane was not as naïve as Mrs. Durand-Deacon and had always been able to see through Haigh's polite, coercive demeanor. When she asked him where Mrs. Durand-Deacon was, he claimed he didn't know. He told her that she didn't show up for their meeting. Mrs. Lane saw through his con; she told him that she didn't believe him and planned to inform the police. Haigh, confident as ever, offered to drive her to the police station himself in his Alvis. Luckily she turned down his offer or she may have ended up dead too.

After two days when Mrs. Durand-Deacon still hadn't returned, Mrs. Lane called the police and reported her missing. She told them that she knew that she had been planning on traveling to Crawley with John Haigh.

When police questioned Haigh, he was as calm and persuasive as ever. Haigh explained that he had planned on meeting Mrs. Durand-Deacon at the Army & Navy Department Store to drive down to Crawley that day. He had waited for her but she didn't show up. He claimed that he made the drive by himself.

Initially, police believed his story and didn't take the disappearance seriously, but when the newspapers heard the story that a rich widow had gone missing, the police took more action and looked closer into John Haigh's story.

When the police checked his background, they quickly realized that Haigh had a long history of fraud and forgery. Haigh was an accomplished con-man. When they went down to his workshop in Crawley, they found that the "factory" that Haigh claimed to have was little more than a shed with a small trashy yard.

Inside the single-room shed they found random tools and rags, but they also found chemicals, a thick rubber apron with stains on it, heavy rubber gloves, a wartime gas mask, empty carboys marked "acid" and heavily corroded metal drums.

They also found the stolen revolver that he had used to kill his victims, a receipt for the sale of jewelry, a handbag, and a dry cleaning receipt for a Persian Lamb Coat. The coat, handbag and jewelry were verified as having belonged to Mrs. Durand-Deacon.

When police pulled Haigh in for a second interview, he was cocky and unconcerned, even dozing off as he waited for the interview to begin. But when police confronted him with the evidence that he had Mrs. Durand-Deacon's possessions, he took a different tone and admitted his horrors.

> "Mrs. Durand-Deacon no longer exists. I have destroyed her with acid. You will find the sludge which remains at Leopold Road. Every trace of her body has gone. How can you prove a murder if there is no body?"

Haigh mistakenly believed that if a body didn't exist, then a murder was unprovable. Not only was he wrong in believing that, but Forensic Pathologist Dr. Keith Simpson found trace amounts of Mrs. Durand-Deacon in the remaining sludge in the yard.

Inside the workshop, they found bloodstains that matched her blood type. This alone was not enough to prove murder, but when they searched through the sludge in the yard, they found three small stones not much larger than olives. These were gallstones covered in fat that had were much more dense than normal human tissue and had not been dissolved by the acid. Additionally, Mrs. Durand-Deacon's false teeth were not dissolved by the acid and were easily linked to her.

On March 2, 1949, police officially charged John Haigh with the murder of Mrs. Durand-Deacon.

Though he had been arrested, he still believed he could not be prosecuted and freely informed police of his murders of the McSwans and the Hendersons. Police did not know of these murders because they had never been reported missing. He confessed to three additional murders as well, including a woman from Eastbourne, another from Hammersmith, and a man named Max. But police were never able to confirm those murders. Haigh told police exactly how he had killed them as well and even claimed to have drunk their blood before dissolving the bodies.

Prosecutors, however, believed that the claims of drinking blood were a ploy to bolster an insanity defense. During the trial he claimed that he had been obsessed with blood since he was a little boy. He described a dream he recalled:

> "I saw before me a forest of crucifixes which gradually turned into trees. At first, there appeared to be dew or rain, dripping from the branches, but as I approached, I realized it was blood. The whole forest began to writhe and the trees, dark and erect, to ooze blood...A man went from each tree catching the blood... When the cup was full, he approached me. 'Drink,' he said, but I was unable to move."

Haigh's plan didn't work. During the trial the prosecution proved that he misunderstood the Latin term "corpus delicti" to mean that a murder conviction is not possible if a body is not found.

On July 13, 1949, the jury only took thirteen minutes to find Haigh guilty and on August 10, 1949 at 9:00 a.m. he was hanged at Wandsworth prison.

Haigh donated his signature green suit and red tie to Madame Tussaud's Wax Museum, which is still on display today in the Chamber of Horrors.

4

THE BLACK WIDOW

T he story of Dena Thompson is quite unbelievable. In retrospect, it's easy to look at the life of her husbands and lovers and wonder how they didn't see through her lies and deceit. But at the moment, it's not quite that easy. Dena Thompson duped man after man, and even a jury. She got away with her crimes for over twenty years before finally landing in prison.

Thompson's first husband fell for her lies and spent three years in hiding, fearing for his life and lost everything he owned. Her third husband thought he had the perfect marriage until one day he was beaten within an inch of his life. Ultimately, they were the lucky ones and escaped with their lives. Her second husband wasn't so lucky.

Dena was born Dena Holmes in 1960 in the north London Town of Hendon, to Michael and Margaret Holmes. Though she was raised in a lower middle class family, her upbringing was, for the most part, normal. She showed no indication of abuse or neglect, and she excelled in school, so it's unclear how she developed her deep hatred of men.

After high school Dena got a job at the Halifax Building Society where she worked as a bank teller. She was working there when she first met Lee Wyatt in 1982. Though their meeting was a blind date, they got along extremely well and the two of them were married after dating for just one year. Five years later they had a son named Darren.

Dena and Lee started a small business they called Denalee Crafts, a combination of their two names, where they made and distributed small stuffed toys. Lee worked full time for their toy business while Dena worked part time and kept a full-time job at the Woolwich Building Society. Though Lee was very passionate about the business and they had hoped to make their fortune selling the toys, the idea just didn't take off as they had hoped.

While placing ads in the West Sussex Gazette for their toys, Dena met a young man named Julian Webb who worked for the newspaper. Though Julian had no idea Dena was married, she had her first taste of infidelity and started an affair with him.

It was becoming increasingly clear to Dena that the toy business was not going to bring her the riches she had hoped for. Lee eventually took a job at a local hotel and Dena found an illegal money-making opportunity without letting her husband know. She began skimming money from the Woolwich Building Society; over time she pilfered the hefty sum of £26,000.

Now that she had a little money of her own, Dena needed to get her husband out of the picture so she could continue her relationship with Julian. To her, the marriage had run its course, and she had lost faith in Lee's ability to make her rich. Her next step was to concoct an elaborate scheme to get rid of him.

Just three months after Dena and Lee had signed the mortgage papers on a new home in Yapton, West Sussex, she put her plan into motion. Dena told Lee that both the airline company Aer Lingus and the Walt Disney Corporation were interested in one of their toys called "Shaun the Leprechaun." It would be a huge deal that would net the two of them several million dollars and set them up for life. Dena even forged a Disney letterhead to make her imaginary contract more believable to Lee.

But there was a setback with the deal. According to Dena, the mafia had got wind of their deal with Disney and wanted in on it. If they didn't get their cut, they would eliminate them and their family. Amazingly, Lee bought all of Dena's lies and grew extremely paranoid that the mafia would come after them at any time.

On June 30, 1991, when a bill collector showed up at the front door, Dena told Lee that it was the mafia at the door and he would need to run out the back door and go into hiding.

Using an unbelievable web of lies, Dena convinced Lee to go into hiding in the small seaside town of Newquay. She somehow convinced him to leave phone messages and write letters to her implicating himself in the fraud that she had committed in the Woolwich Building Society. She said it was the only way to throw off the "G-Men", the fictional name she came up with for the mafia, and she would let him know when the whole thing had blown over and the deal with Disney had finally gone through.

Of course the deal with Disney was a lie and Lee spent the next three years of his life living in poverty and fearing for his life. He managed to find work at an amusement arcade under an assumed name of Colin Mitchel, but sent almost everything he earned back to his wife thinking that it would all be over soon and he would be a multi-millionaire at home with his wife.

Lee had no idea that just six months after he had run out the back door of their home Dena had married another man: Julian Webb. Dena was now married to two men, making her a bigamist.

Dena and Julian Webb

Lena's neighbors were confused when they saw wedding cards in the front window of their home and Julian moving in. They had no idea what had happened to Lee. But they were even more confused when, just after the wedding, they saw other men coming into the home and Dena kissing them on the doorstep. The stream of mysterious male visitors was constant.

It wasn't long before the Woolwich Building Society caught on to her embezzlement. She was being threatened with termination and prosecution if she didn't return the money. Dena made up another elaborate story for her new husband, Julian. She told him they wanted to fire her because she had developed a terminal illness and had taken too many days off of work.

Julian eventually heard about the missing £26,000, but Dena explained that it was her first husband, Lee, that had actually stolen the money. She told Julian that Lee was a violent man who had returned to Yapton and was sending her threatening letters and phone calls. She even claimed that Lee had broken into the home, and had stalked, assaulted, and raped her. She convinced the police to have an injunction put out against Lee, banning him from his own home.

Lee now thought both the mafia and the police were looking for him and showed up at the home while Julian was upstairs asleep. Dena managed to turn him away, but she now knew that it was only a matter of time before her lies would be found out.

The hammer was coming down quickly on Dena, and she needed to act fast. She was terrified that Lee would come home and expose her bigamist marriage, and she was also being taken to court for the missing £26,000.

June 30, 1994 was Julian's thirty-first birthday, and his mother called their home to wish him a happy birthday. Dena answered the phone and explained to his mother that Julian had been sick for the past two days and couldn't speak on the phone. She said he had been out in the sun too long and had drunk too much alcohol.

Julian's mother knew something was wrong because Julian was an avid bodybuilder, religiously working out three days a week at the gym and watching everything he consumed. He didn't drink alcohol at all. He also wasn't the type to spend much time in the sun.

That evening Dena made Julian a large plate of hot curry, his favorite dish. He thought of it as a challenge to eat the hottest curry he could possibly stand and encouraged her to make it hot. Dena seized the opportunity.

The next morning at 1:00 AM Dena called the ambulance when she found that Julian was unresponsive. Julian died from an overdose of dothiepin, an anti-depressant, and aspirin. Dena had spiked the curry with a massive dose. Dena told the police that Julian had been depressed and had committed suicide.

The coroner recorded an "Open Verdict", meaning there was insufficient evidence that Julian had died of a suicide. The Sussex police also determined that there was no proof that the death was suspicious. The investigation was therefore closed.

Early the following morning, Dena was dressed in her nightgown underneath an overcoat, anxiously waiting on the steps of the West Sussex Gazette, where Julian had worked. She was waiting for the manager to get to work. Just hours after her husband was pronounced dead, she stated to his manager,

> "Julian's dead. I need to speak to the advertising manager about the insurance money."

Dena was wasting no time and was hoping to collect on Julian's £35,000 pension plan he had through his employer.

While waiting for his pension money to arrive, Dena was livid to find that Julian's mother had stepped in. His mother was able to prove that Dena was not eligible for the pension because she was not actually the next of kin. She pointed out that Dena was still legally married to Lee Wyatt, her first husband.

Dena's attempts to have Julian's body cremated were also foiled by his mother, who insisted on a burial. This move would come into play years later when the body would need to be exhumed.

Out of spite, Dena wore a revealing, black leather mini-skirt and low-cut blouse to Julian's funeral and waved to the family as she left. It seemed that Dena may have got away with murder.

Lee was still on the run and Dena found herself alone again. The stream of men coming to and from the house continued. One of those men, Robert Waite, had known Dena years earlier just after high school. He received a card in the mail from her inviting him to a reunion party. When he called, Dena invited him out to dinner.

During dinner Dena tried a new story on her latest victim. She told Robert that her late husband was a bodybuilder and had died of an overdose of steroids. She also told him she was dying of a terminal illness and only had months to live. She said it was her dream to go to Florida before she died, knowing that Robert would offer to make her wish come true. Just as she had planned, Robert fell for her trap.

While on their trip to Florida, Robert woke in the hotel room in a daze and felt a sharp prick in his side. He was sure that someone had drugged him as he remembered nothing from the previous day. Out of the blue Dena suddenly told him that she needed to leave. She had to fly up to New York to testify in a trial against the mafia. The truth was that she flew back to the United Kingdom to appear in court for the fraud she had committed against the Woolwich Building Society. Dena left Robert stranded in Florida for three weeks with no money and no way home. Robert was eventually arrested and deported back to Britain.

On August 31, 1995, when Robert returned to the UK, he went to Dena's home to find out what happened to her. That's when he found out they had convicted her of stealing £26,000 from the Woolwich Building Society.

Dena had created a fake identity of a woman named Christina Duke and used that identity to transfer money into an account at the Woolwich Building Society. She would then withdraw the money for herself.

During the trial, police discovered that Dena had scripted the phone calls, threats, and letters from Lee Wyatt specifically to incriminate him. She had coerced him in to believing that he had to do this to protect his family.

Dena's accusations of rape and abuse were also lies. Police discovered that Lee was actually hundreds of miles away in Newquay, living in poverty under an assumed name at the time she claimed she was assaulted.

Dena was sentenced to eighteen months in prison for her crimes, but only served nine months of her sentence and returned to her home in Yapton. The stream of men at Dena's door started again as soon as she arrived. She was attracting the men from ads she had placed in the lonely hearts columns; Richard Thompson was one of them. In her ad, Dena described herself as a "bubbly blonde," and within just a few months of dating, she and Richard got married in a spur-of-the-moment wedding while on a trip to Florida.

Dena told her new husband that she had won the lottery but could only access the money from the United States, so the two of them made plans to immigrate. She encouraged Richard to retire from his job and cash out his pension, then they would combine their assets before they leave. Richard had no reason not to believe her. She lured him with the prospect of owning his own fishing company in Florida after she had received her lottery winnings.

In January 2000, after only a little more than a year of marriage, Dena told Richard that a lawyer would show up with their US Green Cards and they could leave for their new life. But first she had a surprise for him. She was feeling adventurous and wanted a bit of bondage sex to celebrate the event.

Dena locked their German Shepard in another room and told her husband to lie on the floor. She ran a hot bath, then tied his hands behind his back, taped his ankles together, and put a towel over his face.

Richard thought he would be getting something really kinky. What he really got was an aluminum baseball bat to the head. Richard was bleeding profusely, but was still conscious and trying desperately to untie himself. After struggling, he was able to untie himself, but by that time she was stabbing him with a kitchen knife. Unable to see from the blood pouring down his face, Richard reached for her face and pressed his thumbs into her eyes.

"You let go of the knife or I'm gonna put your eye through your head," Richard said.

When it was over, Dena had already cleaned out his bank account, contacted his life insurance companies about selling his £89,000 policy, and had spoken to a real estate agent about putting his house up for sale.

Dena pleaded not guilty when she was arrested for the attempted murder of her third husband, Richard Thompson. She told the court that Richard had flown into a rage when she told him that her story about moving to the United States was all a big lie. She claimed she acted in self-defense and that Richard was the real criminal.

On August 17, 2000 Dena convinced the jury that she was innocent and was acquitted of the attempted murder. She did, however, admit to fifteen counts of deception against Richard and her former lovers. For these crimes, she was found guilty and sentenced to three years and nine months in prison.

The whole ordeal with Richard, however, prompted the Sussex Police to take a closer look at Dena's life. When they saw the way she had taken advantage of all of her boyfriends and husbands, they re-opened the case of the death of Julian Webb. With the family's approval, his body was exhumed, but the examination provided no new evidence.

Police then looked into the various accounts she had given for the night of Julian's death. In a written statement to police, she claimed that she couldn't accurately recall what happened that night. She told some people that Julian hadn't eaten in days, while she told others he had just eaten a hot curry. Police charged her with Julian's murder.

In December 2003 Dena Thompson went on trial for the murder of her second husband, Julian Webb. She was found guilty and sentenced to life in prison with a minimum sentence of sixteen years.

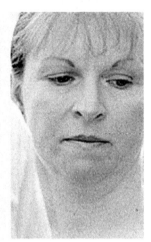

Dena Thompson

After Dena Thompson's conviction, investigators teamed with Interpol to a look at all of her past lovers. They were worried that she may have killed more. Their investigations took them to Bulgaria, where Dena had done much traveling in her late teens and early twenties.

One boyfriend in particular, Stoyan Kostavj, a Bulgarian native, had been reported missing but has never been located.

5

THE BUS STOP KILLER

J ust after 4:00 PM on March 21, 2002, thirteen-year-old Milly Dowler was walking home from school after she and her friend had eaten at a cafe near Walton-on-Thames station in southwest Surrey, England. Her friend boarded a bus for home, and Milly waved goodbye to her as the bus pulled away. Milly then continued on the few remaining steps to her home.

Most of the walk home from the bus stop to Milly's house was covered by CCTV cameras, but a few steps were not covered. This is where she disappeared from all cameras, never to be seen again. Though it was a safe area, she had no idea that a psychotic monster was watching and waiting for her.

By 7:00 p.m. that evening Milly had been reported missing and a massive nationwide search began. Media attention of the missing girl was extensive. They aired a reconstruction of her last movements on the popular BBC show, *Crimewatch*, and *The Sun* newspaper offered a £100,000 reward. The Surrey police offered an additional £50,000 reward to find her, but the rewards only led to an avalanche of false leads.

After six months of no clues, on September 18, 2002, Surrey police announced that the body of Milly Dowler had been found twenty miles away in Yateley Heath Woods in Hampshire. The killer had left her uncovered, savagely beaten, and dumped nude in the woods.

Pollen experts analyzed the foliage that had grown around Milly's remains and were able to estimate that she had been dumped there not long after she had gone missing, probably within a week.

In the first twenty months of the investigation, Surrey police only had one viable clue: after searching through hundreds of hours of security camera footage throughout the area, they noticed a red Daewoo car pulling out of Collingwood Place at around the time Milly had gone missing, but the video was grainy and they were unable to read the license plate number.

In the six years that Emma Mills had lived with her boyfriend, not once had she ever seen him change the sheets on the bed, but on March 22, 2002, one day after Milly Dowler went missing, all the bedding from their bed was gone, including the duvet.

When Emma asked her boyfriend, Levi Bellfield, why he had thrown out the bedding he claimed that the dog had made a mess on the bed and he had to throw all the sheets away.

Emma thought his actions were odd, but what was even more odd was that her little red Daewoo Nexia car was missing. Levi explained that he was out drinking with friends at a pub the night before, had got too drunk, and taken a taxi home. Another first for Levi. But she didn't really think too much about it until the two of them went back to the pub to pick up the car and it was gone. Levi told her that it must have been stolen and left it at that.

Levi Bellfield was born in 1968 in Southwest London. He was a mama's boy to the extreme. After the death of his father when he was ten, Levi began sleeping with his mother in her bed and continued to do so until he was sixteen. According to one of his ex-girlfriends, he would still sleep in the bed with his mother during visits home in his thirties. She also claimed his mother wiped his bottom for him until the age of twelve.

By the time he was sixteen, Levi was still shorter than five feet tall. Frustrated by his tiny size, he took up bodybuilding and started a steroid regime. Though short, the steroids massively increased his size, but that also came with the side-effect of "roid-rage." Bellfield went from a scrawny weakling to an angry 280 pound hulk with a nineteen and a half inch neck.

Levi Bellfield

In school he was notoriously rumored to have tried to have sex with his sister's pet rabbit before ripping its head off, which got him the nicknames "Bugsy" and "Rabbit Fucker." Even to this day, his former classmates refer to him with the monikers on Facebook.

Throughout school his classmates—particularly girls—severely bullied Levi, and he grew to have an extreme hatred for women—blondes in particular. He was known to go through his mother's magazines and scratch out the faces of any blonde females with a knife.

Levi left school when he was sixteen and worked as an auto mechanic. Throughout his life he worked as a bouncer at clubs and pubs around London, bought and sold cars, and also ran his own wheel-clamping business.

As a nightclub bouncer, Levi was known to abuse young girls who wanted entry into nightclubs. He kept a bed in the back of his van and would use ketamine or cocaine to coax the girls into his van to take advantage of them. From 1995 to 2001 many complaints of rape were made by young girls aged fourteen to seventeen, but their memories were hazy from the drugs and there was rarely a conviction.

In his wheel-clamping business, he was notorious for running scams on people by clamping random cars and demanding money to unclamp them.

In one particular scam he would put an ad in a newspaper for a brothel. When the men called, he would set up an appointment for them and give them an address for the girl. When the men arrived and realized the girl didn't exist, they would come back to their car to find a wheel clamped and Levi would be there to collect the money. The men would pay every time because they didn't want to admit that they had plans to visit an escort.

Levi first appeared on the police radar when he was still a child of fourteen for burglary and theft. Over the next twenty years he would build up a huge list of offenses ranging from weapon possession, rape, drug possession, threats to kill, assaulting a police officer, and several violent assaults.

With his business of buying and selling cars, he had access to a vehicle scrapyard, where he could have a car turned into an unrecognizable cube of metal. That was what Levi's girlfriend believed happened to her red Daewoo Nexia, though she wouldn't report it until two years later.

Throughout the years Levi Bellfield fathered eleven children from four separate women. His wives and girlfriends would later describe the savage beatings and the mental manipulation they would have to endure until they were able to get away from him.

Nineteen-year-old Marsha McDonnell had just graduated from high school and was taking a year off so she could travel to Australia before starting university the next year. She had plans to travel in the coming summer.

In February 2003, Marsha had spent the night at the movies with friends and took the 111 bus from Kingston back to her home in Hampton, London. She got off at the Percy Road bus stop just ten doors from her home and started walking down Priory Road. The walk should have taken her no more than five minutes, but she had no idea that a sadistic monster was following the bus in his car waiting for her to get off at the bus stop.

Just forty yards from her home, Marsha's neighbor heard a loud "thud" and rushed outside, where she found Marsha bleeding in the street. Her handbag and cell phone lay next to her body. She had been brutally beaten on the head with a blunt instrument, most likely a hammer, and was hanging onto her life by a thread. Ultimately, the poor young girl didn't stand a chance. She was rushed to the hospital, but died the following day from multiple skull fractures and bleeding around her brain.

Milly Dowler & Marsha McDonnell

At the crime scene there was no evidence of sexual assault, robbery, or a struggle of any kind. It seemed that the killer's only motivation was to extinguish her life.

Though the abduction of Milly Dowler happened less than six miles from where Marsha was murdered and both had their skulls crushed, the two cases weren't linked at the time. Milly's case was being handled by the Surrey police and Marsha had been killed just across the London border along the River Thames, meaning the case would be handled by The Metropolitan Police, the department that handles crimes in the thirty-two boroughs of London.

Similar to the Milly investigation, police examined security camera footage from several sources including footage from inside the bus she was on and cameras located externally on all busses in the area.

One clue garnered from the footage was that of a silver Vauxhall Corsa car. The camera on the front of the bus showed the car passing the bus and pulling into Priory road on the left where it stopped and waited. The footage, however, was grainy and investigators could not accurately identify the license plate number.

Kate Sheedy had been out celebrating the end of final exams with her friends on the night of May 28, 2004. Late that night eighteen-year-old Kate had got off her bus and started the walk toward her house where she lived with her parents.

As she walked up the sidewalk she noticed that a white Toyota passenger van passed her, which came quickly to a stop in a parking spot along the sidewalk ahead of her. The driver turned the lights off, but the engine was still running and the windows were darkly tinted.

It was after midnight and she didn't feel comfortable walking next to the van, so she crossed the street to avoid it and walked along the opposite sidewalk. Her sense that the van seemed suspicious was correct, but that wasn't going to help her. As she passed the van, Levi Bellfield watched her cross the street. He sped toward her and hit her as she crossed the road. Once the van had run over her and was in front of her, he put it in reverse and backed over her again, then sped off into the night.

Amazingly, Kate was still alive. She tried to stand up, but couldn't. She tried to yell for help, but only a whisper came out. She was able to find her cell phone and called police.

999: "Where does it hurt?"

Kate: "Everywhere. The car stopped to check me out. He ran over me again. He just ran over me."

999: "He ran over you again."

Kate: "Yeah"

999: "He ran over you twice?"

Kate: "Yeah... and I really hurt!"

When emergency crews arrived Kate's back was torn open. She had every rib broken, a broken collarbone, a punctured lung, a ruptured spleen, damage to her spine, and her liver had been ripped in two.

She spent the next month in the hospital, most of it in intensive care. She eventually recovered from her injuries but suffered from post-traumatic stress disorder and depression.

The attempted murder of Kate Sheedy happened six miles northwest of Marsha McDonnell's murder and was handled by The Metropolitan Police. Both cases happened to young blonde girls in their teens who had recently got off a bus. Police now suspected that they had a serial killer on their hands.

Despite her injuries, Kate's memory was fully intact, and she was able to give police some helpful details about her attack. She remembered that it was a white passenger van with blacked-out windows, and the driver-side door mirror was broken.

Police went through thousands of hours of security camera footage but didn't see the van. They would later realize that the van had indeed been caught on CCTV, but they had missed it because there was one video tape that had gone undetected. This grave error would allow the killer to attack one last time.

Just three months later on August 19 2004, twenty-two-year-old Amélie Delagrange was having a night out with her friends. She was a French national from a small village in northern France going to school in the UK studying applied languages and working in a bakery. She and her friends were having drinks at Chryztal Wine Bar, and just after 9:30 p.m. she boarded the 267 bus toward home.

Amélie dozed off for a few minutes on the bus ride home and missed her bus stop. On the internal bus camera she was seen asking the bus driver how far back her stop was. When the bus driver told her it was only about a ten-minute walk, she decided to enjoy the summer night air and walk home rather than wait for another bus back.

Like the girls before her, Amélie was a young blonde and had popped up on the predator's radar. As she walked through the large grassy cricket pitch on Twickenham Green, Levi Bellfield followed her into the middle of the field and smashed her head open with a blunt object.

At 10:30 p.m. she was found lying in a pool of her own blood, but still alive. Her handbag and cell phone were missing. Amélie was rushed to the hospital, but died slightly after midnight.

Kate Sheedy & Amélie Delagrange

Police knew that the last three attacks were linked, but at this point they still hadn't linked these attacks to the death of Milly Dowler in Walton-on-Thames, Surrey.

One thing different about this murder was that the killer had taken her handbag and cell phone. Using cell tower activity, investigators tracked the cell phone activity after the attack. They found that Amélie's phone had permanently lost contact with the cell tower about twenty minutes after she was found at the location of Walton-on-Thames. The distance between Walton-on-Thames and Twickenham Green was too far for the killer to have been on foot. He had to have been in a car.

Again, police referred to the CCTV camera footage from inside and outside of Amélie's bus and other busses in the area that may have captured her as she walked back home toward Twickenham Green. The area between Twickenham and Walton-on-Thames was not busy at that time of night, and they were looking for vehicles along that journey.

After searching through more than 2,000 hours of footage, police found what they were looking for. They noticed a white Ford cargo van that had driven the route at that exact time. They had grainy images, but again, couldn't make out any license plate numbers. The footage showed the white van randomly driving around the Twickenham area along side streets for forty-five minutes before the murder. He was clearly hunting for a victim.

Police then enlisted the news media and the public to help in the search for the killer. When they revealed that they were looking for a white Ford cargo van that would have been in that area at the time, Levi Bellfield's ex-partner began to put some clues together.

Johanna Collings had met Levi Bellfield when she was seventeen-years-old and he was working as a bouncer at a club called Rocky's. They started dating four years later and over their years together had two children. Johanna suffered extensive abuse at the hand of Bellfield for years, and despite being separated for five years, she still lived in fear of him and was constantly tormented by his stalking.

Though he was married to Emma Mills at the time, on the night Millie Dowler went missing, Bellfield showed up on Johanna's doorstep crying with blood on his hands. He told her, "I've done something terrible and only God can forgive me," but wouldn't tell her exactly what had happened. It wasn't until the death of two more girls that she put the pieces together.

When Johanna realized that the police were looking for someone with a white Ford cargo van in association with the killings, she knew Levi was responsible.

Johanna went to the police and her information was taken like the thousands of other tips that came in regarding the killings. She explained that Levi owned a white Ford cargo van, lived in the area, and had an extreme hatred for young blonde girls.

Investigators looked into Bellfield's police record. His rap-sheet was extensive, and they noticed that in May 2004 he had been arrested while driving a white Toyota Previa van, the same model of passenger van they were looking for that had run over Kate Sheedy. It even matched her description down to the broken driver's side mirror. Detectives now knew that Bellfield had both a white passenger van and a white cargo van. Two of the exact vehicles they were looking for. When they dug deeper, they found another vehicle link: He had also owned a silver Vauxhall Corsa, the vehicle that was seen in the CCTV footage stalking Marsha McDonnell just before her death.

Police immediately started twenty-four-hour surveillance of Levi Bellfield. During the surveillance, they watched as Bellfield approached and harassed two young girls at a bus stop. After the brief altercation, police asked the girls what he had said to them. They said he asked them how old they were. When they replied that they were fourteen and fifteen he replied to them, "Nice and fresh. I'll bet you are both virgins." The girls then walked away.

After ten days of surveillance police knew they had their man and on the morning of November 20, 2004 moved in to arrest Bellfield on suspicion of the murder of Amélie Delagrange. When the arrest team arrived at his home, it appeared to be empty, but after an extensive search they realized that Bellfield was hiding in the attic, naked under the insulation.

Bellfield & the home where he was arrested

During Bellfield's questioning he replied, "No comment," to every question while calmly yawning and picking his teeth with his fingernails.

When investigators looked further into Bellfield's life, they realized that he was responsible for more mayhem than they had previously known. He was reported to have gone by forty-two different assumed names. During the evidence finding they dealt with twenty-seven investigations for murder, rape, and serious assault. Though they were inundated with the massive number of offenses, prosecutors decided to concentrate on the murder investigations for now.

It wasn't until March 2, 2006, before police had built their evidence and formally charged Bellfield with the murders. There was enough evidence to link him to the murder of Amélie Delagrange and Marsha McDonnell as well as the attempted murder of Kate Sheedy, but they didn't quite have enough to link him to the murder of Millie Dowler yet. His only reply to the charges were, "Not guilty."

Two years later at Bellfield's trial he still denied all charges, but the evidence was overwhelming. On February 25, 2008, Levi Bellfield was found guilty on all three charges—the murder of Amélie Delagrange, the murder of Marsha McDonnell, and the attempted murder of Kate Sheedy. He was sentenced to a whole-life tariff, and the judge recommended that he should never be released from prison.

The murder of thirteen-year-old Milly Dowler had been unsolved for six years, was being handled by the Surrey police; it had never been officially linked to the other murders.

After his conviction, investigators were still looking through Bellfield's files to try to link him to other crimes when they noticed that, at one time, he lived on Collingwood Place in Walton-on-Thames. When they looked up the address they realized the home was literally twenty yards from where Milly Dowler was last seen alive.

The only evidence they had on that murder was the CCTV footage of the red Daewoo Nexia pulling out of Collingwood Place just ten minutes after Milly was last seen. When police realized that Bellfield's wife owned the Daewoo Nexia, it was clear that he was responsible for that murder as well.

In May 2011, Bellfield finally stood trial for the murder of Milly Dowler nine years prior. Again, he was found guilty and seven weeks later was sentenced to another whole-life term.

Bellfield was also charged with the abduction and false imprisonment of seventeen-year-old Anna-Marie Rennie in

2001 and the attempted murder of Irma Dragoshi in 2003, but the jury failed to reach verdicts on those charges.

Johanna Collings later told reporters,

> "I wanted to go to the police so many times, but could never find the courage. I will have to live with the guilt that Milly might still be here today for the rest of my life."

> "Every single day I think if I had opened my mouth maybe her, Marsha McDonnell or Amelie Delagrange wouldn't have been killed."

Further investigation of Levi Bellfield revealed that he had connections to a number other convicted pedophiles. Police believed he may have been part of a gang of pedophiles that were suspected of grooming young girls for child sex. As of 2020 the gang have never been brought to justice.

In 2016 Levi Bellfield converted to Islam and changed his name to Yusuf Rahim. The move is popular with inmates in Britain because it grants them more time outside the cell, better meals, and an excuse to get out of some classes and work detail.

As of January 2020 Levi Bellfield resides in Her Majesty's Prison Frankland in the village of Brasside in County Durham, England. In 2019 he was found in his cell within "minutes from death" and was put on suicide watch.

As with many inmates convicted of sex crimes, Bellfield is repeatedly taunted by other prisoners for his crimes and regularly gets in fights. In 2020 he was deprived of television privileges for fighting with two other inmates.

6

THE SUFFOLK STRANGLER

The Yorkshire Ripper was notorious for his reign of terror that lasted six years and resulted in the deaths of thirteen women. The slightly lesser-known Suffolk Strangler worked much faster. Over the span of just six weeks in 2006, the Suffolk Strangler killed five young prostitutes and terrorized the area around Ipswich, England.

The legality of sex work differs slightly in the United Kingdom from that of the United States. In the UK, the prostitution itself—the act of selling sex for money—is not technically illegal. However, soliciting the sale of sex in a public place, like a street corner, is illegal. "Curb crawling" is also illegal. It is a term used to describe men in cars cruising the streets looking for street-walking prostitutes.

In 2006 Ipswich, England in the county of Suffolk was known for its seedy red-light district. London Road was an area just outside of the city center where young women would stand on street corners waiting for men who were willing to pay for sex. Though it was a small area, there would be approximately 100 girls per night working the streets of Ipswich.

Prostitution wasn't the problem though. The underlying problem in Ipswich was the drug usage. The city was known for a horrific drug problem, and all the girls who walked the streets were addicted to heroin or crack. They were slaves to their addiction and needed quick money to get their next fix. Nineteen-year-old Tania Nicol was one of those girls.

When she was sixteen, Tania left home and moved into a hostel nearby. It was around that time that she was introduced to cocaine and heroin and developed an addiction. By the time she was eighteen she was working at Cleopatra's, a local massage parlor. It wasn't long, however, before Tania was fired. Cleopatra's had a strict no-drug policy, and she was unable to hide her addiction. She then moved back in with her mother and younger brother and turned to the street for work.

Her family knew of her drug problems and tried desperately to help her, but they had no idea she was working as a prostitute, despite frequent phone calls from strange men asking for "Chantelle," the name she was using as a prostitute. Tania had been working the streets for over a year when, on the evening of October 30, 2006, she took the bus into town in order to walk the streets. She never returned.

Tania Nicol

Despite her problems with drugs and prostitution, leaving for days at a time was just not something Tania did. On November 1, Tania's panicked mother reported her missing. Police quickly put out a public appeal to try to locate her, but she seemed to have just disappeared without a trace.

Just like Tania, twenty-five-year-old Gemma Adams was once a bright and bubbly young girl, but fell in with the wrong crowd when she was about seventeen. Over time, she lost contact with her family and succumbed to drugs and prostitution on the street corners of London Road. Gemma had been working as a prostitute for two years; she and her boyfriend, Jon Simpson, were both heroin users.

On the night of November 14, Jon walked Gemma to the red-light district where she worked, as he always did, and went back to their home. Because of her high-risk line of work, Gemma kept in constant contact with her boyfriend and friends even while working. In the early hours of November 15, when Gemma didn't return his text messages, Jon became worried. Like Tania, Gemma wasn't the type to just disappear, and Jon reported her missing.

Gemma Adams

Missing persons in Suffolk weren't unheard of. Police handle about two hundred missing persons per year, but two in a span of two weeks that were both prostitutes working the same few corners began to ring alarm bells with the police. Officers distributed over 20,000 leaflets around the area, set up random roadblocks where they stopped over 500 cars, and interviewed over 2,000 people in regard to the disappearances, but still received no viable leads. Detectives had a sinking feeling they would not find the two girls alive.

In late November there had been significant storms in the Suffolk area that caused flooding. On the morning of December 2, the flooding had receded and a worker at the local fish hatchery was tasked with checking the levels of the lakes, rivers, and streams in the area. As he walked along Belstead Brook near Hintelsham, he came across what he thought was a department store mannequin. As he got closer, he realized it was the naked body of a young woman and immediately called police. When police retrieved the body, they identified it as that of Gemma Adams.

Police believed that the brook was just a dump site and that Gemma had been killed elsewhere. Because of the recent flooding in the area, it appeared that Gemma's body had traveled down the fast-flowing stream, which washed off almost all possible forensic evidence. Additionally, because of the amount of time the body had spent in the water and the amount of decomposition, the pathologist could not accurately determine a cause of death.

With one of the missing girls found dead, police now rushed to find the second one. Their first intuition was to continue searching Belstead Brook, and their hunch was correct. Six days later, as the police dive team searched the brook downstream toward the town of Copdock, they found another nude female body. It was the body of Tania Nicol who had disappeared six weeks earlier.

Like Gemma, Tania's body had been in the water too long and very little forensic evidence was available. The medical examiner again could not determine a cause of death.

Suffolk normally only had about six murders per year, but there had now been two in just six days. Police suspected they had a serial killer on their hands, but were unable to officially connect the two killings because of the lack of forensic evidence.

The news quickly spread to the media, which flocked to the city for around-the-clock news coverage. Panic crept over the area and people felt uneasy traveling the streets by themselves.

Police increased their street presence around the area of the red-light district. The intention was to protect the girls that walked the streets at night, but many of the working girls didn't welcome the protection because it drove away their potential clients. It made them feel safe, but that safety came at a cost for them.

Two days later, on December 10, a man was driving through a wooded street in nearby Nacton and noticed something in the shrubs off to the side of the road. He had actually seen it three days earlier and ignored it, but when he noticed it again, he stopped to look. About thirty yards from the road was the body of yet another naked young female.

The body had been purposely posed on the ground in a cruciform position; on her back with her legs straight and her arms outstretched at a ninety-degree angle as if to form a cross.

Since the body was found a good distance from the road and there were no drag marks, investigators initially suspected that there may have been more than one killer.

Police didn't have any reports of missing girls in the area, so they were unsure of who she was. An autopsy revealed she had been asphyxiated and was about three months pregnant. From the tattoos on her body, police were able to identify her as twenty-four-year-old single mother, Anneli Alderton.

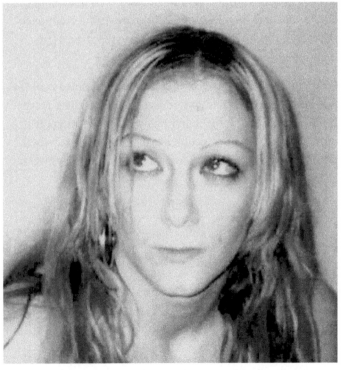

Anneli Alderton

Like the other girls, Anneli had been addicted to drugs since she was sixteen and sold sex on the streets of Ipswich. Since her body was deposited on dry land, the pathologist was able to determine the cause of death: Airway obstruction; she had been strangled.

Though there was still no definitive evidence that the three killings were linked, any doubts they were dealing with a serial killer were soon quashed. Suffolk police was one of the smallest forces in England, and they knew they would need help if they wanted to defeat a serial killer who was killing so rapidly.

There were forty-three police forces in England and Wales; forty of which sent help to Suffolk. Five hundred officers and staff were sent, bringing the total to 1,100, and making it one of the largest manhunts the east of England had ever seen. Over 100 members of the nation's Forensic Science Service came to help as well. But despite the extra help, the torrential rains in the area had washed away most of the evidence.

Using CCTV footage, detectives found that Anneli had traveled on the train to work on the evening that she went missing. The footage was from December 3, the day after Gemma's body was found. That told police that the killer was still killing even after they had increased their presence in the red-light district. The killer thought of himself as invincible.

After the third murder, media from all over the world were covering the story and were camped out in tents on the front lawn of the police buildings; they dubbed the killer "The Suffolk Strangler." Reporters spent time walking the streets of Ipswich and speaking with the working girls. One of the girls they interviewed was twenty-four-year-old Paula Clennell, who chose to work the streets despite the risks because she desperately needed money to support her drug habits.

Reporter: "Why have you decided to come out tonight?"

Paula: "Cause I need the money. I need the money, ya know?"

Reporter: "Despite the dangers."

Paula: "Well, that has made me a bit wary about getting into cars, you know?"

Reporter: "But you will do that tonight?"

Paula: "Well, probably. It would be safer to get a flat and work from there, but it's getting a flat that's the problem."

Paula Clennell

Shortly after the interview with a reporter, two more girls were reported missing. Paula Clennell was one of them, and Annette Nicholls was the other. Paula was last seen on December 8, and Annette was last seen on December 4.

Annette Nicholls

With three girls dead and two more missing, the entire city was now in shock, but the killer was just getting started. Police took advantage of the media presence and requested the help of the public to look for the missing girls.

On December 12, within twenty-four hours of Anneli's body being found, police got another dreadful phone call. A man walking along the old A14 road in Levington had found a naked female body crumpled in the bushes about twenty-five feet from the side of the road.

Within minutes of the call, police had a helicopter in the air and officers on the ground. They arrived on the scene to find the body of Paula Clennell, the girl that had given the interview to reporters just a few days earlier.

The helicopter above was circling around the area as the officers below investigated the scene. It was then that one of the searchers noticed something on the video coming from the helicopter. A few hundred yards up the road was the body of another young girl about thirty feet from the road. Like Anneli, the killer had laid her out naked in a cruciform position with her arms outstretched. Police identified the body as that of the second missing girl, twenty-nine-year-old Annette Nicholls.

A postmortem examination of the bodies revealed that Paula Clennell had died of compression to the neck. Like Anneli, she had been strangled. But the pathologist was unable to determine the manner of death of Annette Nicholls. Though they only had a definite cause of death of two of the five girls, police believed they all died of strangulation by the same killer.

Within a matter of six weeks, five young women had been murdered. All were prostitutes working the same few streets in Ipswich, Suffolk. The killer was on a rampage, and police were at a loss.

The media and the people of Ipswich were in a frenzy with many people afraid to leave their homes. The newspaper, *News of the World*, offered a £250,000 reward for information leading to the arrest of the killer. The public appeals and the media coverage led to a massive number of phone calls. The police force that was already swamped with their investigations needed to research every clue to make sure that nothing slipped through.

One person who several people had called in about was a thirty-seven-year-old supermarket employee named Tom Stevens. Almost all of the prostitutes in the area knew Stevens well, and he knew all five of the victims. He seemed to be drawing attention to himself and had been speaking to the media during the investigation. The prostitutes who knew him described him as creepy, weird, and nosey, wanting to know everything about their personal lives.

When speaking to the press Tom Stevens denied any involvement in the murders, but said:

> "I would have had complete opportunity; the girls would have trusted me so much."

> "If I had blindfolded them and taken them to the edge of a cliff and said take two steps but don't take three - they would have taken the two steps."

> "From the police profiling, a lot of it looks like me. A white man, between twenty-five and forty, knows the area, works quite strange hours."

On December 18, police arrested Tom Stevens on suspicion of the five murders. The detectives' next step was to link any evidence found at the scenes to him.

With the first two killings, the killer had dumped the bodies in a brook that had washed away any potential clues. But with the last three, the killer had been more reckless and dumped the bodies in the woods, leaving the possibility of DNA evidence.

As forensic investigators examined the bodies of the last three victims, they were able to find a sample of DNA from each body, but the samples weren't big enough to develop a full DNA profile. Using a process called polymerase chain reaction (PMR), forensic scientists were able to rapidly make millions of duplicates of the DNA, therefore increasing the size of the sample. With the larger sample, detectives were able to acquire a full DNA profile from each body. All three contained the DNA of the same man.

Tom Stevens willingly gave a sample of his DNA, but it didn't match the DNA that was found on the three victims. Stevens was not their killer and was released without charge.

The DNA profile was then fed into the national DNA database where it came up with a match. It matched the record of a forty-eight-year-old forklift driver, Steven Wright. His address was 79 London Road in Ipswich, right in the center of the red-light district; he had only moved to that address a few weeks before the first girl had gone missing. Detectives put him under twenty-four-hour surveillance.

Steven Wright

Steven Wright only had one offense on his police record: Five years prior he was deeply in debt and had a gambling problem. He was working as a bartender at The Brook Hotel where he was caught stealing £80 from the till and was arrested for theft. Because of that arrest, his DNA was in the national DNA database.

Just two days after Tom Stevens had been arrested and released, police arrested Steven Wright at his home in the early morning hours of December 19. The arrest came as a complete shock to his family and girlfriend, Pam.

During Wright's interrogation, police questioned him and asked why they had found his DNA on the naked bodies of Paula Clennell, Anneli Alderton, and Annette Nicholls. During eight hours of interviews Wright replied with nothing more than, "No comment." Generally when a suspect is wrongfully accused of a crime, they will naturally defend themselves. Wright's lack of cooperation was hardly the reaction of an innocent man, but DNA on the bodies wouldn't be enough to convict him. Police needed much more evidence, and they had their work cut out. They needed to look deep into Steven Wright's background and his movements on the nights the girls went missing in order to build a case against him.

At first glance, Steven Wright was a seemingly ordinary, middle-aged man. He didn't fit the stereotypical profile of a serial killer. He was employed, had a relationship, and was forty-eight years old. Most serial killers are in their twenties or early thirties. Statistically, forty-eight is a very late age to get started as a serial killer.

Police believed that Wright's ordinary looks could have been a reason why the prostitutes trusted him and got into his car despite all the warnings.

As a young man, Steven Wright was a dishwasher in the Merchant Navy where he met his first wife and moved to Wales. Using his Navy experience, at twenty-two years old he got a job as a ship steward on the Queen Elizabeth 2 cruise ship.

It was during this time that Wright first began using prostitutes in the various ports of call throughout the world.

While sailing the seas on the QE2 for six years, his first marriage fell apart and in 1984 he met Diane Cole, another crew member on the ship. Though Diane later described him as violent, possessive, and erratic, the two dated and were eventually married and moved to Norwich, England where they managed a pub called The Ferry Boat Inn, which was located in the red-light district of Norwich, and Wright continued his hobby of spending time with prostitutes. He was a regular curb-crawler, and some prostitutes claimed he was into cross-dressing.

During his years in Norwich there were two unsolved murders of prostitutes. Both girls had been strangled and found dumped in woodlands. Two more prostitutes were reported missing but never found. Police began to ask whether Wright may have started his killing years before.

But because Wright had frequented sex workers all of his life, prosecutors knew that his defense could easily use that to explain why his DNA was found on the victim's bodies.

In order to find more evidence against Wright, police painstakingly studied over 10,000 hours of security camera footage throughout the Ipswich area. They were looking for any video footage of Wright or the girls on the nights that they went missing.

Their first finding was footage of Annette Nicholls three days before she disappeared in Ipswich, then Gemma Adams from November 4. They also found footage of Tania Nicol and Anneli Alderton shortly before they had gone missing.

The video footage by themselves wasn't much help though, without being able to place Steven Wright in the same areas at the same time.

Using CCTV and the automatic number plate readers placed throughout the town, investigators mapped the movements of Steven Wright's dark blue Ford Mondeo on the same nights.

Through the CCTV footage police could see that Wright was a regular curb-crawler and had been stopped a few times for soliciting prostitutes, but released without charge. He had even passed through a police road check and answered a questionnaire during their search for the girls.

Wright's girlfriend, Pam, worked nights and police confirmed that she was at work on the nights that each of the girls went missing, giving Wright the opportunity to cruise the town looking for victims.

Following the movements of Wright's Ford Mondeo on CCTV, they could see Tania Nicol entering the passenger side of the car just after midnight on October 30, the day she went missing. Using additional CCTV footage and times of his location in the town, police could see that he was in the proximity when one other girl went missing.

Though they could prove that he was most likely the last person seen with at least two of the girls, that still wouldn't be enough to convict him. It was well known that he had frequented prostitutes for years, and he could still easily use that as his defense.

The police had the DNA evidence to link Wright to the last three victims, but Gemma Adams and Tania Nicol were both found in fast-running water with any DNA evidence long washed away.

Because of the flooding, the hair of both girls was filled with debris—over two pounds of silt, leaves, and vegetation was pulled from each girl. Forensic scientists spent several weeks filtering out the debris from the hair when they found a black nylon fiber in Tania's hair. When this nylon fiber was compared to the fabric from the carpet in Wright's Ford Mondeo, it was microscopically similar. They also determined that the fiber was transferred into her hair by forceful and sustained contact with the carpet. This meant that at some point he had pushed her head onto the floor or trunk of his car with tremendous force.

When police searched Wright's home, they found a pair of work gloves. Forensic tests of the gloves showed DNA from all three of the girls that had been found on dry land. They also found a reflective jacket in his home with spatters of blood that were matched to Paula Clennell and Annette Nicholls. Additionally, fabric from Wright's home was found on four of the five bodies.

More and more evidence continued to pile up. On the body of Annette Nicholls, forensic scientists found a fake fur fiber. The same fiber was also found inside Wright's car. Also from Wright's car, investigators found tiny flakes of blood that belonged to Paula Clennell.

Prosecutors now believed they had enough evidence to get a murder conviction and were ready to move forward with a trial.

Wright had claimed he was innocent, but as the evidence piled up, even his family were losing faith in him. His father went to the prison to visit him, but Wright refused to see him. When his father sent him a letter Wright responded:

> "My head seems to be all over the place at the moment, so please try and sort this out. I know you are a proud man and don't like backing down, but you are the only one that can sort this out. You say you want to help so please do that one thing for me."

The letter went on to explain an unhappy childhood.

> "…you have never seen me angry before because I am a quite(sic) and placid person. whenever I get upset I tend to bury it deep inside which I suppose it is not a healthy thing to do because the more I do that, the more withdrawn I become because I have seen so much anger and violence in my childhood to last anyone a lifetime
>
> But what really makes me sad is the fact that I thought all the family were behind me."

Wright's father knew nothing about his unhappiness, anger, or violence in his life.

The trial started January 14, 2008. During the proceedings he maintained his innocence and said very little. Several weeks into the trial, Wright took the stand in his own defense. The prosecutor presented him with fifty-seven points of evidence over a two-hour session. His only reply to each was, "It would seem so, yes," "it would appear so, yes," or "if you say so, yes."

> Prosecutor: "There are a number of coincidences in this case, aren't there, Mr. Wright? Let's consider a few, shall we? You selected five women from the streets of Ipswich, and on your own account they all died very shortly after they left your company. Is that a coincidence?"

> Wright: "It would seem so, yes."

> Prosecutor: "You selected five women from the streets of Ipswich in the order in which they died. Is that coincidence?"

> Wright: "It would seem so, yes."

> Prosecutor: "It would seem that in terms of picking up prostitutes in Ipswich, you have been singularly unfortunate."

> Wright: "It would seem so, yes."

> Prosecutor: "There are further coincidences, are there not? Shall we start with your DNA? That's another coincidence, isn't it?"

> Wright: "It would seem so, yes."

> Prosecutor: "It would seem your full DNA profile is on the bodies of the three women who were recovered from dry land. Is that a coincidence?"

> Wright: "It would seem so, yes."

Wright's girlfriend, Pam, had testified that she was working at a call center on the nights of all five girls going missing.

Prosecutor: "There would appear to be a correspondence in terms of the disappearance of each of these five women with your partner's work patterns."

Wright: "It would seem so, yes."

Wright moved to the red-light district just weeks before Tania, the first girl, disappeared on October 30.

Prosecutor: "These women went missing during the same period."

Wright: "It would appear so, yes."

Prosecutor: "If these five women were indeed murdered, they were murdered by someone or other during the time you were picking up prostitutes off the streets of Ipswich."

Wright: "It would appear so, yes."

The prosecutor explained to the court that CCTV cameras showed Wright in his dark blue Ford Mondeo leaving the Ipswich area shortly after Tania and Anneli disappeared.

Prosecutor: "Is it a coincidence?"

Wright: "If you say so, yes."

The prosecutor asked about Anneli's body having been posed like a crucifix.

Prosecutor: "Somebody has laid out her body, posing her body."

Wright: "If you say so."

Prosecutor: "Your DNA, a full profile, is on her right breast and nipple."

Wright: "If you say so."

Prosecutor: "You dumped her body there having killed her, didn't you?"

Wright: "No, I did not."

Prosecutor: "The fact is that there are no coincidences, are there, Mr. Wright? The fact is that you murdered each of these women."

Wright: "No, I did not."

This line of questioning went on for two hours detailing fifty-seven separate evidential claims, with Wright claiming that fibers from his car, blood from two of the girls on his jacket, and all the CCTV footage were all unfortunate coincidences. His defense was not very convincing.

The jury adjourned for only six hours before coming back with a guilty verdict on all five counts of murder. As they led Wright from the court, crowds of people yelled at the convicted murderer who had terrorized their city.

Wright was sentenced to life imprisonment with a recommendation of no parole.

His father wrote to him one last time in hope of some sort of explanation from his son.

"Myself, I don't believe and can't even imagine how any one person could have carried out five murders in so short a time. And quite honestly, I don't think you could even kill a rabbit. Well, Steve, that's it for me now. If I get nothing from you, then I believe you are telling me something. Something I'd rather not hear. Love Dad."

His father got no reply.

———

Though it was believed that Wright began his killing spree in his late forties, questions still remained about the missing prostitutes from Norwich when he managed a pub in the red-light district there.

Though police believe they have eliminated him as a suspect in those cases, some criminalists have their doubts. Those four cases remain unsolved to this day.

⑦

BONUS CHAPTER: JAMES PATTERSON

This chapter is a free bonus chapter from True Crime Case Histories: Volume 1

O n an April afternoon in 1996, a man calmly walked into a Manchester police station in England to report that his girlfriend had accidentally drowned in his bathtub. The man was forty-eight-year-old James Patterson Smith and his girlfriend was just a seventeen-year-old child. The truth was that Smith was a sadistic, controlling psychopath and not only had the girl drowned, but she had been subjected to three weeks of some of the most brutal torture England had ever seen. The horrific crime scene brought seasoned police officers to tears.

Kelly Anne Bates was mature for her age. At age fourteen when Kelly told her parents, Margaret and Tommy Bates, that she had a boyfriend, they thought nothing of it. As any parent would, they assumed it was a teenage crush with a young boy from school.

Wanting to raise their children with a sense of independence, they gave Kelly a long leash and let her see her boyfriend as she pleased. It wasn't long before Kelly started staying out overnight and her worried parents called police. When Kelly finally came home, she told them she was staying at her friend Rachel's house, but her parents had a sinking feeling that her story wasn't true.

Kelly Anne Bates

They weren't the only one concerned about Kelly's whereabouts. Even though they had never met him, Kelly's boyfriend "Dave" would occasionally call to ask where she was. What her parents didn't realize at the time was that Dave was already tightening his control around Kelly.

Kelly managed to keep her parents from meeting Dave for a full two years, until she was sixteen years old. That's when she informed them she was dropping out of school and moving in with him. Her parents were livid and called social services and the police for help. Because Kelly was now sixteen, according to UK laws the authorities couldn't do anything. Kelly's parents demanded to meet her boyfriend, Dave.

When Margaret and Tommy finally met him, they were shocked to find that Dave was not a boy but a full-grown man. Kelly and Dave told her parents that he was thirty-two years old, but even that wasn't true. They later found out he was actually forty-eight - older than Kelly's father at the time.

Dave's age wasn't the only thing they were hiding from her parents. Dave was not "Dave" at all. His name was actually James Patterson Smith.

James Patterson Smith

Though mature for her age, Kelly was still young and naïve. She was flattered to have an older man so interested in her, but what she didn't realize was that their relationship was more about power and control than love. Smith controlled everything the young girl did from this point on.

Kelly's demeanor slowly changed. She was no longer the bright, bubbly girl that her mother knew, and they gradually saw less and less of her. When she did show up at her parents' home, she seemed to be troubled and depressed, but refused to admit anything was wrong.

Kelly would show up with bruises on her arms and face. When she showed up with the whole side of her face black from bruising, her parents' concerns reached a new level.

Kelly lied to her mother and told her that she was jumped by a group of girls that beat her up. Each time she showed up with new injuries, her story would change. Her parents had no idea that Smith had a long history of violence towards young women.

Margaret could clearly see this was abuse and went to the police, who told her to make an appointment with a doctor and get Kelly to go in for an exam, so they could document the abuse. But again, Kelly was sixteen and considered an adult. Her mother was helpless. Unless Kelly went in of her own accord, there was nothing that could be done.

Kelly's mother could see that the violence was escalating when Kelly showed up with a horrible bite mark on her arm. Again, Kelly shrugged it off and said that she fell and caught her arm on a chain-link fence.

In November 1995, Margaret pleaded with her to leave Smith, but this seemed to anger Kelly. She then told her mother she would be seeing much less of her. That was actually the last time Margaret saw Kelly alive.

Over the following months, Kelly phoned her mother and told her that she had gotten a job at a factory and was working long hours and weekends; that was why she hadn't come around. Eventually, the phone calls stopped.

In March 1996, Margaret got a Mother's Day card and a birthday card for her father, Tommy. Both were clearly not written in Kelly's handwriting. Smith was now in complete control and toying with them.

On April 17, 1996, James Patterson Smith walked into the Gorton Police Department and reported that his girlfriend had drowned in his bathtub. Police arrived to a horrific bloodbath that was obviously much more than a drowning.

Seventeen-year-old Kelly Anne Bates had indeed drowned in the bathtub, but she had also been held prisoner for at least three weeks and suffered torture beyond imagination.

The pathologist's report revealed 150 separate injuries, including having her eyes gouged out, stab wounds inside her eye sockets, and the mutilation of her mouth, ears, nose, and genitalia. Her head was partially scalped, she was scalded with boiling water, burned with a hot iron, stabbed and cut with knives, forks, pruning shears, and scissors, and her knees had been kicked in.

Literally every room in the house had traces of Kelly's blood. Evidence revealed that she had been tied to a radiator by her hair and her eyes were gouged out at least a week before her death. She had not received water for several days and had been starved, having lost about forty-five pounds.

Investigations revealed that there was a progressive pattern with Smith. They found that he had been married years before and divorced due to his violence against his wife. After the divorce, he dated a twenty-year-old who testified that he used her as a "punching bag" even while she was pregnant. Their relationship ended when he tried to drown her. After that, he had a relationship with a fifteen-year-old girl who testified that he held her head underwater.

At the trial, Smith denied the murder charges and believed he was justified in his torture. Smith claimed that Kelly taunted him about the death of his mother and that she only had herself to blame. He also claimed she had, "a habit of hurting herself to make it look worse on me." When asked why he gouged her eyes out, he said, "She dared me to do it."

The jury didn't even need a full hour to come back with a guilty verdict. The evidence and photos seen at the trial were so horrific that, after the trial, the jury was offered psychological counseling. Every jury member accepted.

James Patterson Smith was sentenced to life imprisonment with a minimum term of twenty years. Kelly was buried the day before her eighteenth birthday.

———

Thank you for reading this bonus chapter. Please check out the rest of True Crime Case Histories: Volume 1 on Amazon.

http://truecrimecasehistories.com/book1/

Also by Jason Neal

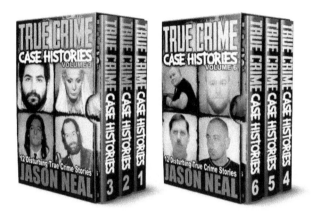

Looking for more true crime books?? I am constantly adding new volumes of True Crime Case Histories. All books are available in Kindle, paperback, hardcover, and audiobooks.

Check out the complete series on Amazon:

US: http://truecrime.page/amazonUS
UK: http://truecrime.page/amazonUK

Choose Your Free True Crime Audiobook

Add Audible Narration and Keep the Story Going!
Plus Get a FREE True Crime Audiobook!

Switch between listening to an audiobook and reading on your Kindle. **Plus choose your first audiobook for FREE!**

http://truecrime.page/AudibleUS

http://truecrime.page/AudibleUK

Lightning Source UK Ltd.
Milton Keynes UK
UKHW011328080223
416610UK00017B/2354

9 781956 566086

ABOUT THE AUTHOR

Jason Neal is a Best-Selling American True Crime Author living in Arizona with his Turkish/British wife. Jason started his writing career in 1989 as a music industry publisher and wrote his first true crime collection in 2019.

As a boy growing up in the Eighties just south of Seattle, Jason became fascinated with true crime stories after hearing the news of the Green River Killer so close to his home. Over the coming years he would read everything he could get his hands on about true crime and serial killers.

Now in his forties, Jason began to assemble stories of the crimes that have fascinated him most throughout his life. He's especially intrigued by cases solved by sheer luck, amazing police work, and groundbreaking technology like early DNA cases and more recently reverse genealogy.

facebook.com/jasonnealauthor

goodreads.com/jasonneal

bookbub.com/profile/jason-neal

amazon.com/author/jason-neal

instagram.com/jasonneal.author